INCLUSION
Issues and Perspectives

INCLUSION

ISSUES AND PERSPECTIVES

(For Teachers, Teachers' Educators and Parents)

Edited by:

KRISHNA MAITRA

VANDANA SAXENA

KANISHKA PUBLISHERS, DISTRIBUTORS

NEW DELHI-110 002

KANISHKA PUBLISHERS, DISTRIBUTORS
4697/5-21A, Ansari Road, Daryaganj
New Delhi -110 002
Phones : 2327 0497, 232 8 8285
Fax : 011-2328 8285
E-mail : kanishka_publishing@yahoo.co.in
kanishkabooks@gmail.com

Inclusion: Issues and Perspectives

First Published-2008

Edition-2024

ISBN : 978-81-8457-030-4

PRINTED IN INDIA

Published by Madan Sachdeva for Kanishka Publishers, Distributors, 4697/5-21A, Ansari Road, Daryaganj, New Delhi-110002, Typeset by Sunshine Graphics, Delhi, and Printed at G.S. Printers, Delhi.

Preface

Pressure has always been on government of the day to take the issue of Inclusion seriously. In spite of many acts passed by the government of different political hues, the scenario regarding admission, retention, continuation to the higher education and job opportunities has not changed much in favour of children with special needs. My association with different organizations, which are running either special or an integrated set-up, strengthened my conviction that Inclusion is the need of the hour. Our department admits students with challenges in its different programmes but not all of us are oriented to needed pedagogy for inclusion. The department offers courses on special education at B.Ed, M.Ed and at M.phil level. It has enrolled quite a number of scholars at M.phil and at Ph.D level to pursue their research in this area. There is an added dimension to this. The department has now given affiliation to Blind Relief Association and Lady Irwin College to run B.Ed Special Education course.

The moment has arrived for taking initiatives in the direction of dissemination of ideas and plans for the future move in the area of Inclusion. In the year 2006, we organized the first one-day seminar on "Inclusion" in the department under the chairmanship of Prof. U.S. Sharma. We had speakers from various institutes like Amar Jyoti, NIMH, Tamanna, Jamia Millia, and Blind Relief Association. Vice-Chancellor, University of Delhi, Prof Deepak Pental, graced the occasion and inaugurated the seminar. The keynote speaker was Dr. Uma Tuli, Ex-Chief Commissioner for Persons with Disabilities GOI and the founder member of Amar Jyoti Charitable Trust. Other distinguished speakers were Prof. S.R. Mittal from Jamia Millia Islamia, Dr. Shyma Chona from Tamanna, Dr. S. Grover from NIMH and Dr. S. Sanyal from Blind Relief Association.

Dr. Thakur, the chairperson of NCTE delivered the validictory address. The response generated by the seminar prompted us to organize the second seminar on Inclusion in the year 2007. We had speakers from a broad array of institutions including NGOs. It was a real pleasure to have a broader perspective as the speakers included academicians, researchers and entrepreneurs who are working with the challenged people themselves at the ground level. Prof. Janak Verma from NCERT delivered the Inaugural Address and Dr. Anupam Ahuja enthralled the audience with her keynote speech. Every other speaker made the seminar really memorable. Dr. Aswini Aggarwal, Joint Secretary of NAB, Dr. Rita Malhotra from Amar Jyoti, Dr. Swati Sanyal from Blind Relief Association, Dr. Usha Sharma from SCERT as well as Ms. Rashmi Paliwal from Balloons made the occasion very special. In this monograph we have attempted to bring together the issues and the perspectives presented and discussed by ours speakers. It was possible only because of the assistance and cooperation I have received from my colleagues and students. They are not only helped in organizing the seminar but also in crafting the content of this publication to its true spirit very faithfully.

I acknowledge the contribution of Ms. Dipi Pathak for administrative coordination during both the seminars. I also acknowledge technical support rendered by Mr. D.S. Chandi and Mr. I.S. Rawat for the same. I express my sincere gratitude to Mrs. Pratibha Goel, Ms. Yukti Gosain and Dr. Jyoti Sharma for doing transcription job of most of the documents and to my dear colleague Dr. Vandana Saxena for supervising the whole process of publication.

I want to express my special thanks to Prof. Bharati Baveja, Head and Dean, Department of Education, University of Delhi, for supporting us in organizing the seminar. She was a guiding force for all of us throughout the project.

I sincerely hope that this publication will be of immense help to those who are working in the area of inclusion.

Prof. Krishna Maitra
Department of Education
University of Delhi
Delhi-7

Contents

PART–I
Policy Perspective

1

Inclusion: Looking Back and Forth

Dr. Uma Tuli

Inclusion is all about mainstreaming education by removing barriers at bringing all children together in school irrespective of their physical and mental abilities. India has over 1000 million people. Of these 200 million are school children and 20 million requiring special needs education. While the national average of gross enrolment in school is over 90 per cent, less than five per cent of children with disabilities are in school. Around 40 per cent children are not able to complete five years of basic education and another 20 per cent leave before completing the further three years of free and compulsory schooling as mandated by the Constitution. The reality presented, is an area of great concern.

The goal of education for children with or without special needs is to prepare them for a happy, productive and useful civil life. Indian literature is full of educational thinkers and visionaries who have questioned the capacity and relevance of modern schools in imparting education. Earlier, children with disabilities had been receiving education in separate schools called special schools. Special schools were opened for different type of disabilities. It has now been advocated that disabled children should be educated in main stream schools in the company of non-disabled peers.

Perspectives on the disabled and on their education have been changing. It also brings in sympathy, compassion and humanitarian approach towards disability. But, these children need support and opportunities instead of compassion and sympathy. This perspective on disability gives foundation for a new form of education that would neither require a child to get isolated nor fit in the regular school system not designed for her, hence, gives the origin of the concept of *Inclusive Education,* where the school responds to the ability of the child. In simple terms, inclusive education means that all children, including those with disabilities learn together in mainstream neighbourhood schools. Inclusion is a process by which a school expands its resources to meet the learning needs, physical needs and emotional needs of all the children. There are various models of education working in the system.

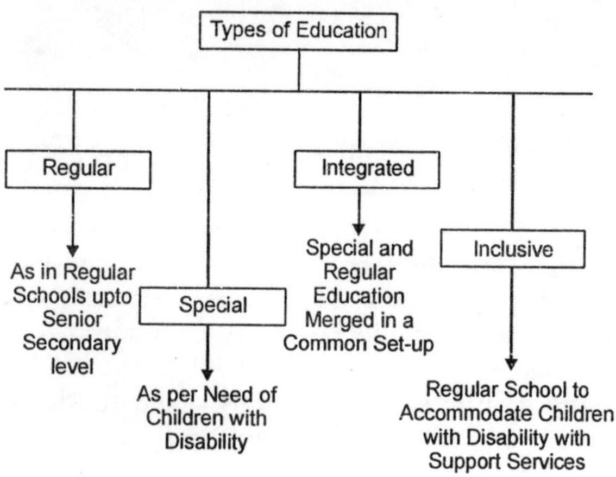

Although inclusion is increasingly catching attention of policy makers, it is yet to find the place in the perception of society. Inclusive education is different from integrated education. It is expanding the scope of education to all children in regular schools. Also, it focuses on improving the education system so that it could include all children, that means, children with disabilities must have access to regular schools which can accommodate them within the child centered curriculum capable of meeting their needs.

All children are special in one way or another. A teacher in the classroom is confronted with the job of identifying these needs, to assess their precise nature and to provide learning experiences accordingly. It is a natural feeling that individuals or groups of individuals should not be written off, marginalized, left out of things, cut off from their fellows or sidelined. This feeling goes along with, or is constituted by both a sense of justice and a sense of compassion. Often it is connected with the idea of equality, or fraternity, or human rights, or even democracy. For bringing the disabled and disadvantaged closer to the school, it is important to remove the barrier by bringing the concept of inclusion.

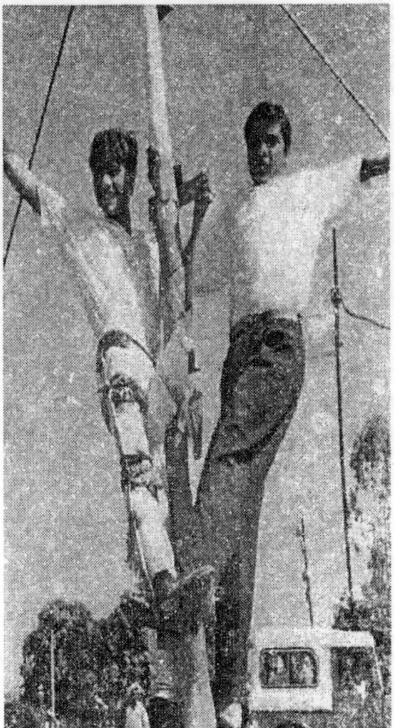

The philosophy of inclusive education rests on giving equal opportunities to an integrated group of able bodied and differently abled children studying together. It refers to the "opportunity for persons with a disability to participate fully in all of the educational, employment, consumer, recreational, community and domestic activities that typify every society" – (ILSMH, 1994). Inclusive education changes attitudes. It produces a meaningful voice in the world of silence, brings a ray of hope in the life of those who live in darkness. It also lends helping hands and understanding to those who need love and concern. It enables children with special needs to reach their potential and live with equality and dignity.

Vision of Inclusive Education

Inclusive education embodies set of components that encompasses the needs, expectations and aspirations of all children including disabled.

- Equal opportunities.
- Effective educational programmes.
- Assistive devices.
- Support services.
- Age-appropriate classes.
- Neighbourhood schools.
- Parents involvement.

Inclusive education is the most effective means to sensitize:

- Students learn to appreciate each other's unique strengths and abilities.
- Students are encouraged to help each other.
- Students with disabilities are able to foster friendships in a natural manner and in a natural environment.
- Non-disabled students get a chance to develop positive attitudes toward people with differences.
- Self-esteem and a feeling of achievement comes automatically.
- Students often learn desirable social behaviours best from each other, in a typical environment.

Challenges in Inclusive Education

Inclusive education cannot be implemented in the present situation. There are various challenges ahead:

- Social attitude towards disability.
- Lack of awareness.
- Scarcity of trained teachers.
- Absence of barrier-free built environment.
- Scarcity of proper learning material.
- Resistance of parents.

Inclusive education is not a utopian philosophy. Indian education system has an approach to educating the disabled that educationists recommend as inclusive pedagogy. The Government of India has passed three legislation for education and rehabilitation of disabled children:

> The act is significant in the sense that it requires the appropriate government and local authorities to ensure that every child with a disability has access to free education in an appropriate environment till he/she attains the age of 18 years.

For education and rehabilitation of these children, the Government of India has three Legislations on Disability:

- The Rehabilitation Council of India Act, 1992.
- The National Trust for the Welfare of Persons with Autism Cerebral Palsy, Mental Retardation and Multiple Disabilities Act, 1999.
- The Persons with Disabilities (Equal Opportunities, Protection of Rights and Full Participation) Act, 1995.

The Act also has provision under Section 39:

- Reservation of 3 per cent seats in Educational Institutions.
- Free education upto the age of 18 years.
- Training of teachers in management of disabilities.

- Barrier free access infrastructure.
- Appropriate reading and teaching/learning material.
- Encourage non-formal education.

Implementators of Inclusive Education in India

- National Institute of Educational Planning and Administration.
- District Institutions of Education and Training.
- State Institute of Education Management and Training.
- District Primary Education Programme.
- Project Integrated Education for the Disabled.
- National Institute of Open Schooling.
- Indira Gandhi National Open University.
- State Council of Education Research and Training.
- Sarva Shiksha Abhiyaan through Ministry of HRD.
- Special Education through Ministry of Social Justice and Empowerment.
- Various NGOs.

Two major initiatives taken by the government for achieving the goals of universalisation of elementary education, namely D.P.E.P. and S.S.A. have accepted integration of children with disabilities in main stream schools as a commitment. D.P.E.P. has been making several interventions to achieve its objectives towards integration which includes community mobilization, early detection, in-service teacher training, resource support etc.

Children Enrolled in Regular Schools as a Result of Interventions

Andhra Pradesh	:	17,067	Meghalaya	:	1,070
Mizoram	:	638	Chandigarh	:	296
Goa	:	2,164	D & N Haveli	:	603
J & K	:	15,488	Tripura	:	2,522
Gujarat	:	26,731	Karnataka	:	27,040
Maharashtra	:	1,39,000	Punjab	:	30,000
Delhi	:	30,000	Madhya Pradesh	:	1,10,000
Nagaland	:	1154	Tamil Nadu	:	59,560
Uttar Pradesh	:	2,19,059			

The office of CCPD has brought out *booklets* on mainstreaming of children with disabilities. States/UTs have been requested to get the same translated into respective regional languages. There are several institutions in India who have successfully experimented both integrated as well as inclusive education.

Education with a Difference at Amar Jyoti

Inclusive Education

Medical Centre

Vocational Training

Capacity Building Courses

Community Based Rehabilitation

Self-Employment

Trained Teachers

Assistive Devices

Barrier Free Environment

Child Guidance Centre

Academics

From Tears to Smiles

Pioneered in taking education beyond the textbook by including medical care, vocational training, sports, cultural and co-curricular activities. This holistic approach is today the norm worldwide.

- Extended education to the mentally challenges through social inclusion strategy
- Home training and promotion of self-help group programme for parents of children with disability.
- Equal number of children with and without disability study together.
- Introduced movement therapy in collaboration with Recreational Sports Development and Stimulation–Disabled International (RESPO DS-DI), Netherlands.
- Conducting capacity building courses to constantly upgrade skills of teachers.
- Creative art therapy strategies for the intellectually challenged and other children.

Result!!

Each child at school has a smile of content...

Many other schools all over India are including children with disability not only as per 3 per cent legislation but as the school's commitment to civil society in the country. The Spastics Society of Northern India prepares children with spasticity for inclusion in regular schools at pre-school level. Counselling is provided to the children, parents and school authorities so that beneficiaries do not have any problem in mainstreaming at regular schools. The Laxman Public School in Delhi is successfully facing the challenges of dealing with the challenged. Swami Shivanand's Bhawan, renders similar pre-school training for mainstreaming at his centre in Delhi with successful results of communication disorder cases. The Delhi Public School has a special section for mentally challenged and the Principal also runs a special school "Tamanna", for the intellectually impaired.

The integration of visually impaired at a couple of institutions like the Blind Persons Association in Ahmedabad aims at "Changing what it means to be blind." Bharatiya Vidya Bhawan in Delhi has special sections for mentally challenged in their regular secondary school. Akshay Prathisthan in Delhi is implementing the concept of mainstreaming through inclusive education, vocational training and medical care.

According to Vidya Sagar Institute—Chennai, inclusion is:

To be a part and not stand apart
To belong and not to be isolated
To be accepted and not accommodated
To have friends and not just companions
To feel needed and not just a person with needs
To be a participant and not a spectator
To have responsibilities and not just enjoy rights
To have opportunities and not favours
Is to be really "Included".

Equal Responsibilities Alone can Lead to Equal Opportunities—Partners in Action—Effective Inclusive Education

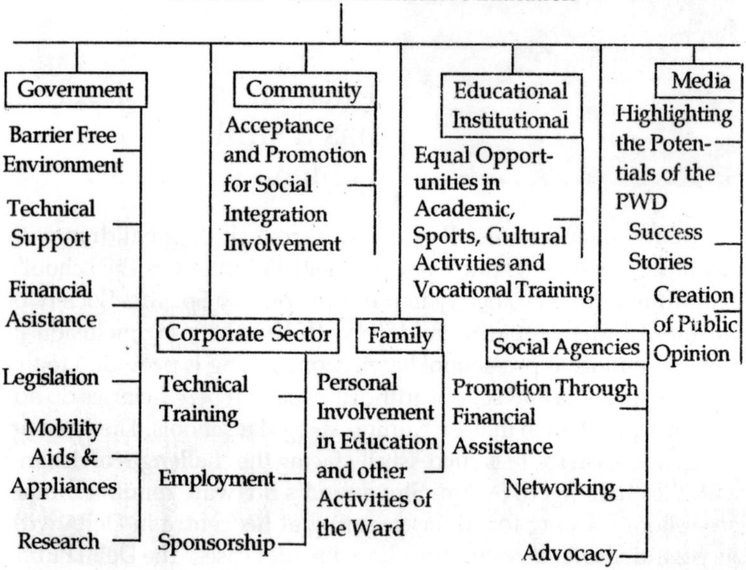

Vidya Sagar believes that the needs of people with or without disabilities are the same. Ultimate aim is to create an environment that allow every individual from childhood to grow together respecting the differences.

The inclusion movement needs vision of child centered approach, inclusion strategies, like whole class inclusion teaching, peer tutoring, activity based learning, organising support for diversity. It is to socially integrate the disabled children. There may be special sessions for academics but bringing them together for social and co-curricular activities should be encouraged.

Suggested Activities

- Leadership for campaign to ensure that every child with disability attends regular/special school or home based education programme.
- Survey to identify children with disabilities particularly those not enrolled–follow up with enrolment.
- Bridge education to facilitate enrolment.
- Scholarship for students with disabilities. Free books, uniforms also to be made available.
- Aids and appliances to be provided to those needing them.

For bringing the disabled and disadvantaged closer to the school, it is important to make barrier free environment. Let us work together to create inclusive society. We should always remember:

Inclusion is a journey not a destination.
It is difficult but achievable.

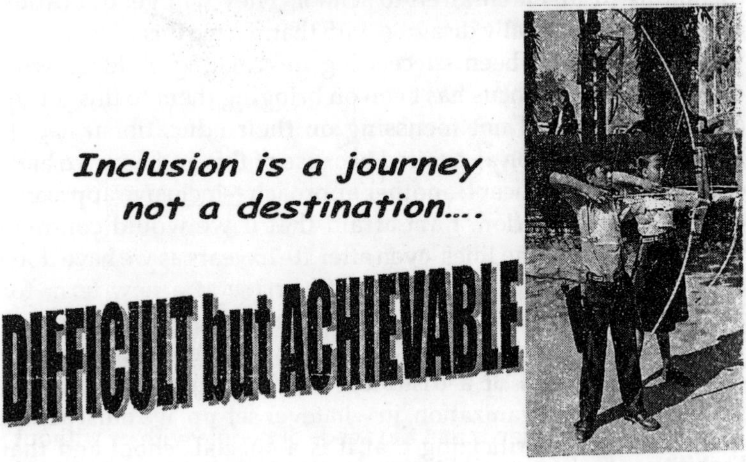

2

Role of RCI in Promoting Education of Children with Special Needs

Prof. S.R. Mittal

I will be sharing my views out of my experience and whatever I have been gaining by interaction with my students and other professionals in this field of special education, both in India and in other countries. I will talk not as an academician lecturer on inclusive education but I will give my views on inclusion. I will also present few strategies and attempts that are being made particularly by RCI towards promoting education of children with disabilities and special needs.

When we say inclusion of children with disabilities in mainstream, and by that what I mean is bringing them to school. The focus is on 'bringing them to school'.

I read in a book published 2-3 years ago, where it is said, 'Bring the disabled children to school. They will get education automatically.' I totally disagree with that. To me this is the reason why we have not been succeeding in reaching children with disabilities as our focus has been on bringing them to this set-up or that set-up and not focussing on their educational needs. Integrated education also failed because of this and now we have come to another concept, another approach – inclusive approach, or inclusive education. I am afraid that if we would continue thinking on the same lines even after 10-15 years as we have done about integrated education, we will arrive at a new term for inclusive education and we will find another term hereafter. Therefore, my submission is that we should keep in mind that if educational needs of a disabled child are being met by an institution or an organization, in whatever set-up, we must accept that; rather than criticizing that it is a special school and that here the student is not getting this or that. If the student is getting education, then he/she is getting empowered, and we must accept that programme.

Secondly, it is also a fact that a debate has always been there as to, 'who should be going to which type of school?' There should be no debate. It is a very simple phenomenon that all disabled children will never be included in mainstream education. They have not been, even in the most developed nations like US, Canada and so on and so forth. In USA, they don't even talk about inclusive education. In their Disability Act, they have said that education of children with disabilities or special needs should be in the least restrictive environment. I do not know, what do they mean by 'least restrictive environment?' For learning of a given child with disabilities, if a special school is suitable for him let it be the ideal place for his education; if a regular school is suitable for him let it be an ideal system; if integrated education/semi set-up is ideal for him then that is the right approach for him.

America is a country where there is no lack of resources whereas we are short of resources. We aspire that with this shortage of resources, we must find some ways by which we can reach all children with disabilities.

Friends, Education is becoming more and more expensive. The situation was different earlier, but now it is not so and if education for the non-disabled is expensive, how can education for the disabled be different, anyway.

In 'Sarva Shiksha Abhiyaan' Rs. 1200 p.a. were earmarked for education of children with disability per child. In a school, where no facility exists, you give the headmaster Rs. 1200 p.a. for the education of that child. What will the poor headmaster do with that Rs.1200? Will he be able to get any improvement for him? Can he provide any training to the teachers with Rs. 1200?

Therefore, the approach which is necessary will have to be— 'Develop the disabilities in different settings and not in one setting' and that is the reason also why PWD Act has not perhaps talked of any particular setting. The only thing that is said in the Act is that most appropriate environment for the education of children with disabilities should be ensured. It has not said that it should be integrated environment. The term 'inclusive' was not in use at that time in 1995; it is the invention of the 21st century. Therefore, the approach can be and should be what RCI has thought of. They have developed strategies for reaching children with disabilities.

The first strategy for promoting education of disabled children that should be adopted is that input about special educational needs of children with mild disabilities should go to all general teacher education programmes, whether it is a diploma course for nursery school teachers, or elementary school teachers, whether it is B.Ed. or M.Ed.

For this purpose, they had constituted a committee to identify areas from different disabilities and how to incorporate them in general diploma, B.Ed. and M.Ed. programmes. RCI has completed the work and NCTE is in the process of incorporating these components in general teacher education programmes which will then be circulated to all the universities and institutions which are offering these courses for incorporation. NCTE or RCI cannot impose anything on universities and other institutions because these are autonomous bodies. But RCI can certainly lay down certain guidelines which universities are bound to follow, therefore, input is likely to be passed on to the universities by NCTE very shortly.

The second thing that the RCI has done and developed is the launch of a foundation course on disability. This course is of duration of 3 months and all in-service teachers are eligible to enrol in this course. Out of the 90 days programme, 15 days have been earmarked for contact programme in which basic inputs relating to the educational needs of children with disabilities are given and rest is through distance mode. For this purpose, they have even developed modular content and content details. And they are providing these to interested institutions free of cost, but those who participate or enrol in this foundation courses will have to pay Rs. 1500, and this sum will have to be paid either by the teacher himself/herself or by his or her school or by the State Government. Many State Governments have come forward to invest and spend this money to get their teachers oriented for meeting the educational needs of students with disabilities. For example, Tamil Nadu, Kerela, West Bengal, Maharashtra and Gujarat have come forward and they are spending money to get their regular school teachers oriented in disability.

The third thing that the RCI has done is that it has developed a credit accumulation system of training of teachers. As one school may have a student with blindness, another student might be there in the same school with mild mental retardation and there may be third child with hearing impairment. One cannot afford to have three special educators and if the degree of disability of these three children is of profound nature especially of hearing impairment and blindness, then a general teacher will never be able to fulfil their educational needs. In the initial stage one will need to have support of a special educator. So, no school can afford to have three special teachers.

NCERT had made an experiment in late 80's and early 90's of having a multi- category teacher training course of one year duration. The evaluation of that project, under which that course was developed, says that that idea could not materialize and succeed because of many reasons. The main reason being that in one year it is not possible to give all that is essential for a teacher to be able to handle all children with different disabilities.

Therefore, the RCI has developed credit accumulation system where those who have done, say, B.Ed. Special Education (Visual Impairment) but want to acquire skills in mental retardation or hearing impairment, can acquire that at a session of, say 6 months or 4 months, through distance mode; complete that module and they could be registered as special educators for mental retardation also. If they complete another module, they will be registered as special educators for hearing impairment also. Thus, RCI hopes that if this system is implemented with sincerity within a period of, say, 5 to 6 years, many teachers will be available in the country who will be able to handle children with different disabilities especially in the four major disabilities areas—visual, hearing, mental retardation and locomotor impairment.

The next strategy that the RCI has tried out is the launch of Distance Education Mode. I have never been a supporter, and am still not a supporter, of Distance Education in preparation of teachers for children with disability needing special education, because special educator needs lots of skills in Braille, sign language, use of special equipments and so on and so forth. Through distance mode you can give theory but you cannot teach skills.

But because RCI has thought and found it useful, it has launched a programme in 2001-02 through MPBOU (Bhoj Open University). It is a course for B.Ed. in special education through distance mode wherein they have identified certain centres all over the country as study centres. Students enrol themselves there and attend three contact programme in the entire period and in that they are given training in skills. Rest of the teaching is through distance mode for which, it has developed relevant material also. Many people can question the quality of material but then improvement can always be done. The material available can be used anywhere for teachers.

The next strategy of RCI is that it has started awareness generation regarding disability, rehabilitation or education of disabled children which is an important step in this area. For this purpose, it has launched, in collaboration with IGNOU, since last year a one hour teleconferencing programme every week. For this, it has established Distance Receiving System (DRS) in about 50 or 60 places in the country, where people can gather and interact with experts through telephone during that one hour. Different topics of importance in the field of education of disabled children are dealt with by experts of that particular topic.

So these are some of the strategies through which the RCI has been trying to reach children with disabilities, in whatever setting possible. It says, and I also believe, that inclusive education is possible and desirable on one single ground only that ultimately persons with disabilities have to live with non-disabled. Nowhere in the world isolation of disabled for entire life has been contemplated or has been possible.

One attempt was made in Holland, where a village for only persons with disabilities was created but that also failed. I don't know whether you have read or heard of it or not. I went to Holland three or four years ago and asked many people whether they had heard of that village, before I went to Holland, I was curious to go and see that village which was thought of being only for disabled. It has not possible. Disabled have to live with non-disabled. And when they have to live with non-disabled, why not from the very beginning itself?

But if we want to keep them in the mainstream from the very beginning, we have to make a concerted effort. And most important is that all teachers must be trained, given proper understanding about disabilities and skills that they need, in order to teach children with disabilities. This is the first requirement that I consider is the most important for realising inclusion.

The second thing that I consider important to make the inclusion of disabled work is the availability of all the teaching-learning material including textbooks in accessible formats for children with disabilities. If a blind child is there, textbooks in Braille should be available. If a hearing impaired child is there, facilities for teaching science to him should be available. Other teaching-learning material should also be available.

Third thing is parental orientation. Parents have a major role to play in the education of their children. After all, children stay in school with teachers for just 5-6 hours. They spend 18-19 hours with their parents only and parents have to play an important role in the education of their children. But parents of disabled children are not aware of how to handle them? Therefore, they also have to be oriented in taking care of their children with disabilities. These are the three major challenges that I consider of great importance.

Fourth thing that I want to share with you is the environmental modification of the school campuses. All schools whether they are public schools or other type of schools, should be accessible to all children with disabilities whether they are visually impaired or have locomotors impairment.

Please never think that all children can ever be able to come to mainstream education. First assess the child, consider the child's degree of disability and his needs. Keeping his degree of disability in mind, decide whether he has to be placed in inclusive setting/ education, mainstream education or some other alternative method or system will have to be provided to him. There can be no single option/approach, which can meet the needs of all children with disabilities.

Issues Raised

On Parental Education

RCI has developed a 6 months course for the parents, which will be launched very shortly in about 2-3 months time through distance mode. Material is ready in each disability area which is to be given to parents. Out of these 6 months, there will be 2 contact programmes also, for parents of children with disabilities and other parents too. These contact programmes will be run by NGOs and other institutions. NGOs will be given material free of cost. For other facilities NGOs will have to bear the cost. Yesterday in RCI, I was told that 300 NGOs in the country have agreed to run this contact programme for the parents wherein they will be oriented. If they have a one year-old child, what symptoms, things they must keep in mind or look for to be able to know whether their child has any disability or difficulty. What symptoms they should look for. Where should they go if the child is declared disabled. What they should do. How they should take care of his needs at that particular age. All these things are included in that material which RCI and IGNOU have jointly developed. That material will be given free of cost to those institutions which will be launching this course.

On Teacher-Training Programme, Job Opportunities

In Jamia, we are having two courses at the B.Ed. and the M.Ed. levels. By and large, we are following RCI syllabus except condensing it into 6 papers because our general B.Ed. is of 6 theory papers and 2 types of practical teaching and other practical work. We have modified the syllabus for that very purpose.

In B.Ed., we are offering 4 papers along with papers on visual impairment and learning disabilities in whichever one wants to specialize. Our students in the past have been receptive. They have learnt many things during these courses here in Jamia and our students who have offered learning disabilities have been accepted by the USA and are working there. Some of them are working in public schools. One student who did her B.Ed. Special Education (Learning Disabilities) and thereafter M.Ed. also, is working in British school in Delhi only. And other public schools are also accepting them. They are doing well. The only problem is, as you know, all these public schools look for English as medium of instruction. And most of the students, who come for special education, do not have good English communicative skills due to which they find it difficult to get job in public schools. And apart from public schools there is no scope for students offering learning disabilities at B.Ed. or M.Ed. level. So far as students offering visual impairment, many of the teachers are accepted in institutions working for the visual impaired like National Association for the Blind, Delhi.

On RCI's Very Restrictive Role of Categorisation

Needs of gifted and talented children have never been marginalized in our society, or anywhere else. Disabled children have been marginalized and RCI is basically constituted to look into the educational problems of children with disability, therefore RCI has not done anything on this matter so far.

The second question, which is relating to children with learning difficulties, dyslexia, dyscalculia and dysgraphia, RCI has developed a course curriculum for B.Ed. (Learning Disabilities) also and the support they provide by way of some material on teaching children with Learning Disabilities. But as all of you know Learning Disabilities or Learning difficulty are not included in the legislative framework. In our PWD Act, Learning Disabilities are not included. And I would like to share one thing with you whether you would agree with me or not is a different issue, but when this law was being formulated in 1994-95, I asked my teacher, my director Mr. Advani, whose name is known to many of you but not to all of you, that why we have not included Learning Disabilities in this. His answer was that it is very difficult to identify a child with learning disabilities. It is very easy to label a child with the label of learning disability. Therefore, learning disabilities have not been included in the act. Even now, in the amendments which are under consideration of the government, learning disabilities are under separate provision. Separate act and legislative framework may be there but not mixing with these facilities which are included in PWD Act.

I will give you an example, I have a friend of mine working in this very university itself, I won't name the department and the name of this lady. She has a son and her son was, as he is the only son and in our families only son means what, you all know how pampered the son or the child is, which results into his poor performance in academics learning. One lady told her to show to a person who is an expert in leaning disabilities which means that it is assumed that he is learning disabled child. Friends, he has no learning disability/

difficulty. Only he was an attention seeker child and he started getting that attention from his parents. He is doing well, he has cleared 10th without any support with good percentage of 71 per cent. All children don't get 90-95 per cent; there are children who get 70 per cent. And if they get 70 per cent we label them as learning disabled. This is total injustice. Theretore, RCI has not taken learning disabled issue very seriously. They have done some work on this front also.

On Material Related to Subject Teaching

So far as lack of material for teaching these subjects like mathematics, science and geography is concerned, in these fields, there is a lack of material, no doubt, but that is only in our country and that too in only northern states. In southern and western states, it is not so. This situation is because of two reasons. Number one, previously as people had obtained exemption from learning mathematics and science. People think when there is an exemption, why should we make efforts to teach it or learn it. Where there is no exemption, these subjects are taught.

It is always said in this field that 100 per cent content of mathematics and science may not be possible for blind children. I will only talk about blind children and not other disabilities. In curriculum upto the tenth standard, 95-97 per cent curriculum can be transacted with some assistive devices and teaching-learning material whether it is of science, whether it is of maths or geography. It is simply because of exemption that people have not been trying to teach these subjects to blind children. I will give you an example, here in Delhi itself there is an institution—National Association for the Blind, R.K. Puram, which is running its own kind of inclusive education, that is children go to regular school, public and government in the morning, and in the afternoon they are given coaching on assistance in areas where they could not understand properly in regular schools. They tell their children that they would have to offer maths and science as other children offer in tenth class. The children resisted and they even threatened to go to the court but the organization stuck to its stand that if you want to remain in this institution, you will have to offer and now, maths and science are taught and their students are getting marks upto 70-75 per cent. They learnt mathematics and science.

Of course, enough material is not there but earlier about 20 years ago there was not even a Braille mathematics course. It is available now. 20 years ago, there were not special geometry kits; they are available at NIVH and other institutions. Now there are talking equipments, not being manufactured in this country, but available in the market. People are going for them. For example, colour recognisers, talking thermometers, talking barometers etc. They are little expensive but some institutions have them, and with the help of these, many things can be taught. You know, in education of the blind, we follow four principles basically. Omission is the last principle. Modification, substitution and duplication are the other three. Omission is the last principle for something that is completely impossible, which is totally visual and without the visual ability, you cannot learn experience, or understand. But as I said, upto tenth standard, 90-95 per cent curriculum can be transacted. Beyond tenth standard also, mathematics and science, not in our country, but elsewhere in the world, blind people do study till PG level. Like in US or UK, in India also there are one or two blind persons who have done Masters in mathematics, PhD. also.

On Teaching Science (Optics)

I said in the beginning that there is a shortage of material; I never said that all material is available. Ninety per cent content area can be taught; if an innovative teacher is there, he can teach light concepts, but learning outcome cannot be 100 per cent same as in case of a sighted child. No one claims that, even the greatest educationist in the field of education of the blind, Nowen Fred himself said that 'learning of blind in many cases may not be similar to that of a seeing child'. But still, some learning of those concepts will be there and they will be able to understand.

On Policies of Government

So far as policies are concerned, there is no shortage, there are lots of policies, everything is there but political will is not there. Policies are just made and declared, I will tell you how PWD Act was passed. On the last day of Parliament session, this Act was presented in 1995, and the MPs thought there was no need to have a discussion on it, and it was passed and it was enacted on 1st January. It is the only Act enacted on 1st January; all other acts have been enacted on some other day. There is no shortage of policies but there is shortcoming in implementation of policies. Our country has limited resources and with limitation of resources, we want to achieve everything. That is not possible. The concept of Education for All, or health for that matter, is a dangerous concept. We are not being able to do anything because of this concept of For-All.

3

Promoting Inclusion Preventing Exclusion

Dr. Usha Grover

Inclusive education is the process of addressing learner's needs within the "Mainstream" school, using all available resources to create opportunities to learn in preparing for life. The emphasis is on reviewing schools and systems and changing them rather than trying to change students.

The Constitution of India has formulated legislative policies to provide for the education of the population with difference which promote inclusive education.

Article 29 (2)

Provides that no citizen shall be denied admission into any educational institution maintained by the state or receiving aids out of the state funds on ground of religion, race, caste, language or any of them. The right is guaranteed to disabled as much as to the non-disabled.

Article 45

Directs the state to provide free and compulsory education for all the children (including the disabled) until they attain age of 14 years.

National Policy on Education (NPE, 1986)

To achieve the goal of 'Education for All' the Government of India has brought education of the group of children for special attention as part of its concern for equalization of education opportunities. The (NPE, 1986) focuses on the needs of children with disabilities. It recommends an integrated education in general schools for children with Locomotor handicaps and with other mild disabilities, orientation and pre-service training of general teachers to meet special needs of these children, provision of vocational training, establish new special schools for severely disabled children and encouragement of voluntary organizations in these tasks.

Programme of Action (PoA)

Formulated for implementing the NPE suggested a pragmatic placement principle. It postulated that the child with disabilities who can be educated in a general school should be educated in a general school only and not in a special school. Even those children who are initially admitted to special schools for training in plus curriculum skills should be transferred to general schools once they acquire daily living skills, communication skills and basic academic skills.

Integrated Education for Disabled Children (IEDC)

The Ministry of Human Resources Development, Department of Education has formulated a scheme known as Integrated Education for Disabled Children (IEDC), which purports to provide educational opportunities for disabled children in regular schools. The objective is to integrate the disabled with the general community at all levels as an equal partners and to prepare them for normal growth and also to provide 100 per cent financial assistance to states in addition to other added facilities such as setting up the resource room, assessment room.

Project Integrated Education for Disabled (PIED)

The Project Integrated Education for Disabled (PIED) was designed to strengthen the implementation of the IEDC. It is being implemented in 27 states and over 22,000 schools benefiting more than 9,50,000 disabled children.

The Persons with Disabilities (Equal Opportunities, Protection of Rights and Full Participation) Act, 1995

The Act is guided by the philosophy of empowering persons with disabilities. The endeavour of the Act has been to introduce an instrument for promoting equality and participation of persons with disability on the one hand, and eliminating discriminations of all kinds, on the other.

National Trust Act (National Trust for the Welfare of Persons with Autism, Cerebral Palsy, Mental Retardation and Multiple Disability), 1999

A landmark legislatiom, this trust seeks to protect and promote the rights of persons who within the disability sector, have been even more marginalized than others. The salient features are:

- First of its kind in the category of persons addressed.
- Recognition of range of independence in skills, daily living and financial management.
- Protection – dominant, rather than autonomy – dominant.
- Local Level Committee – District Level Coverage.
- Decision-making powers to Persons with Disabilities
- Legal Guardianship – Even for parents.
- Stakeholdership of Registered Organsations.

Biwako Millennium Framework

As per the Biwako Millennium framework for action towards an inclusive, barrier free and rights-based society for persons with disabilities in Asia and the Pacific, early intervention and education is one of the 7 priority areas to be focused during the second Asian and Pacific decade of disabled persons (2003-2012). The recommendations made in education was focus of enrolment of Children With Special Needs (CWSN) as schools are resistant to admitting most (CWSN).

Sarva Shiksha Abhiyaan

- (SSA, 2002) endeavours to achieve universal elementary education for all of satisfactory quality by 2010.
- All the policies have distinctly given a mandate of education of the disabled in integrated settings.
- Inclusive education is now part of official policy.

The movement of including students with handicaps in the regular school has received tremendous legislative, financial, research based support not only in India but also all over the world. Time and again Indian constitution has formulated policies, which guarantee the education of the handicapped with that of the non-handicapped group. But taking into view all the legislative policies research based support, financial incentives human rights framework – the movement towards inclusion of children with special needs in the regular education settings does not seem to have gathered the momentum as it should have.

If inclusive education has to become a reality we need to emphasize more on implementation than spreading awareness about the need for inclusive education and formulating policies. In my experience the following ingredients are essential for making inclusion a successful experience.

Ingredients for Successful Inclusion

I—Infrastructure

Infrastructure should be such that creates barrier free environment for everyone.

N--National Level Policies

We have national level policies as discussed above but the need of the hour is to have more policies to implement inclusive education.

- D.P.E.P
- Sarva Shiksha Abhiyaan
- U.N.D.P. Project
- More Policies to Implement Inclusive Education

C—Capacity Building

Capacity building personnel is very much required. Development of competences in persons involved in inclusion i.e. teachers, concerned personnel in Government department policy makers, administrative staff and others staff in ordinary schools and families of persons with disability, peers and community at large is very important for making inclusive education successful. Teachers should master the skills for curriculum adaptation, should be able to develop readiness skills in persons with disability. Above all they should have the commitment and belief in inclusive education apart from being innovative. More training courses for inclusion should be implemented. Bachelor in rehabilitation therapy in one such example, the course is being offered at NIMH, Regional Centre, New Delhi.

L—Legislation Reforms

PD Act (1995), emphasis appropriate educational placement of children with disabilities based on their needs, which demands that a suitable system be developed to include children to regular school.

U—Understanding

Positive attitude and flexibility may be inculcated. Seamless educational provision may be provided.

S—Sensitization

Sensitization of administrators, parents, principals, teachers, drivers and ayahs should be taken as a goal, which needs to be achieved. Administration will focus on the cost of effectiveness of proposed system. Teacher will focus on ways and means of developing effective curriculum and instructional. Peers will show interests in accommodating the child with disability.

I—Initiative

Of all concerned

O—Organization

Every child can be part of inclusive education through careful planning and systematic organization, Children with M.R. can form part of inclusive education by using NIMH package, pre-school package for inclusion and package for children with learning problems.

N—Networking of the following is a must for Successful Inclusion

- NGO's
- General Education
- Ministeries
- Central Governments
- State Governments
- Existing Resources and Models.

Making education inclusive is challenging task, but not impossible. This can be achieved only if the above ingredients are present in the right quantity in a timely manner.

What Needs to be Done?

- Inclusion requires the education system suitable, for children with special needs and not expecting the child fitting into the education system.

- Ainscow pointed out "What is needed are strategies that personalize teaching rather than individualize the lesson." This would mean getting away from following IEPs for special children within classrooms by developing new methods that can stimulate and support participation of all children in the class.
- Success in inclusion lies in efficiency of teacher to involve children in the class rather than the disability.
- Teacher education programme in the country needs fresh look. It is necessary to rethink and revise the existing teacher education course content in order to prepare the teachers to respond to wide range of needs in the classroom.
- Curricular adaptations/modifications in training for inclusive education.
- Improving quality of classroom learning.

Training of all Teachers for Education for All

- Need for research.
- Constituting an Association for Inclusive Education (A platform for sharing knowledge and experience).
- Sharing "Best Practices in Inclusion" initiated by NGOs.
- Success stories to be seen as models and not as exceptions.
- To meet the need to diverse social and cultural multiple models are required.
- B.Ed. for general teacher, Anganwadi worker training, nursery school teacher training, Montessori teacher training etc., the curricular should have input on "Inclusive education."
- RCI has recently signed a memorandum with National Council of Teacher Education, which is a significant milestone.
- Planning and implementing Bachelor and Diploma level courses in inclusive education. Implementing "credit system", modules.
- Training through Distance Mode.

In conclusion, the global aim of education is that everyone has right to education so inclusion is likely to be achieved if inclusive practices are regarded as "not out of the ordinary, but simply as a goal of education."

4

Teacher Preparation for Promoting Inclusion

Dr. Janak Verma

Introduction

Education is seen as a human right in today's context. As it concerns with reform in education, it goes without saying that it is related to restructuring of existing education system. Are we really providing quality education to each child in our schools? Is our education system responsive to the individual needs of all children in the classroom? What are we doing to achieve this goal, is a matter of great concern for all educationists and policy makers of government of all nations. It is about addressing diversity in the classroom. It is about reorientation of teacher education curriculum both at the elementary and the secondary level.

Teacher preparation has to come at the centre stage to bring this reform. It is the teacher who is supposed to address the individual needs of children in the classroom by bringing quality in education. If quality can be brought in our classroom, education can be made responsive to the individual needs of all children. Each child's need has to be met by the teacher because it is the human right of the child to get quality education in schools.

Jomtien Conference set the goal for *Education for All* (1990). It was adopted by Salamanca Statement and Framework for Action on Special Needs Education (1994). It envisages the fundamental policy shift required to promote the approach of inclusive education, namely *enabling schools to serve All Children, particularly those with special educational needs*. Education of Children with Special Needs cannot be achieved in isolation. *It has to be an integral part of general education system.*

Policy

Before we proceed further we must understand as to what is our policy for the education of children with special needs.

At the National Level

The Constitution of India (26 November, 1949) states that everyone has the right to equality of education and of opportunity. The 86th Amendment to the Constitution has reiterated the need for Free, Compulsory and Universal Elementary Education as a Fundamental Right for all Children from 6-14 years. The 93rd Amendment of the Constitution of India has made education a *Fundamental Human Right* for children in the age group of 6-14 years of age and they need to be brought under the fold of education. This includes children with Special Needs. National Policy on Education (NPE) 1986 and its Programme of Action (1992) stressed the *need for integrating children with special needs in general education system.* The objective is *to integrate them with general communities at all levels as equal partners, to prepare them for normal growth and to enable them to face life with courage and confidence.* The children with special needs, who are placed in special schools initially for preparation would also get integrated in common schools once they acquire the communication, mobility and daily living skills.

The Persons with Disabilities PWD Act, 1995 (Equal Opportunities, Protection of Rights and Full Participation) reaffirmed the access to free education to every child with disability in an appropriate environment till she/he achieves the age of 18 years. We have Sarva Shiksha Abhiyaan. It has set time bound targets for achievement of UEE by 2010. This is possible only if the needs of children with special needs are fully addressed in the mainstream education and all children get the opportunity to go to their neighbourhood schools. We also have IEDC scheme. In order to achieve the target of Education for All, Government of India sponsored a centrally sponsored scheme of Integrated Education for Disabled Children (IEDC). It purports to *provide educational opportunities for children with Special needs in common schools, to facilitate their retention and achievement in the school system.*

Now we are moving towards inclusion, which means that all learners and young people with or without special needs are able to learn together in same schools with appropriate network of support services. It aims at providing quality education to all learners in regular schools. It is a matter of human rights for 'All Children'. It is a reform in the existing education system that is meant for all children. It has a challenge for teachers, teacher educators and policy makers to reform and reframe their thinking about education of children with special needs.

Magnitude of the Problem

Indian population has crossed one billion. As per the Sixth all India Educational Survey, the estimated enrolment of all classes under different age groups comes to approximately 130 million from the age group of 4 to 14 years. It may be seen from the following figure:

Estimated Child Population Under Different Age Groups in Millions

Area	*4 to 6 yrs*	*6 to 11 yrs*	*11 to 14 yrs*	*Total*
Rural	10.6	59.1	22.9	92.6
Urban	4.2	19.6	12.9	36.7
Total	14.8	78.7	35.8	129.3
				351 – *7th survey*

The number of children with special needs, according to the figures provided by the WHO, is 2-3 per cent. In terms of Indian population this figure touches to 20 to 30 million children having different types of disabilities.

Teacher Preparation for Achieving the Target of Inclusion

To achieve the target of Education for All, Teacher Preparation is to be given the topmost priority. General Teacher Education System has to be enriched to meet the individual needs of All Children including children with special needs. We need to move a step forward towards inclusive schooling and schools for all, schools that respect the diverse needs of All Children. All in service as well as pre-service teachers need to be geared to address the individual needs of children in the classrooms. For this,

- Teachers need to be helped to accommodate Pupils' diversity in their classrooms.

- Teacher Education needs to contribute to this process.

We need to look in a different way, a way, which is broader and wider. It is about widening our gaze or changing our perception about the education of Children with Special needs. Teachers need to understand that all children can be educated in the existing general education system. We need to consider that difficulties in learning arise as a result of the ways the schools operate. The aim should be to restructure schooling in ways that will make it more responsive to pupils' diversity. Teacher development and capacity building of teachers is to be highlighted. There is a necessity to increase flexibility in curriculum practices and training methods in mainstream classroom in order to be more responsive to the needs of all children.

How can Teacher Education help Individual Pupils to Learn?

In order to make teaching responsive to the needs of all children, teachers should know the ways by which they can help individual pupil to learn. They need to change their attitude towards the education of children of special needs. They need to follow the new approach.

The New Approach

The new approach assumes that difficulties in learning arise because of the interaction of a whole range of factors, some of which lie within children and others connected with the decisions made by teachers. The recognition of this fact leads us to an optimistic frame of mind. It reminds us that what teachers do, the decisions they make, the experiences they provide and the relationships they have with their pupils, all have a major influence on children's learning. All children are special children. The aim must be to respond to all pupils as individuals, recognizing individuality as something to be respected. Instead of providing separate learning experiences for a group of special children, schools need to find ways of offering a curriculum that takes account of individual needs. In other words, the aim must be to make all teaching more effective in order that all pupils can participate in and can have the advantage of the same range of curriculum opportunities. Support should be available as teachers attempt to develop their practice. Collaboration and sharing are important features of successful schools. We should use all resources to achieve the successful teaching-learning situation.

Meeting Individual Needs

Teachers need to be trained in practicing co-operative teaching learning strategies because children learn better in schools where there is a good social relationship. Environment of collaboration helps learning. If parents and members of the community are made equal partners with school, children learn better.

Positive Relationship among Teachers, Pupils, Parents and Community

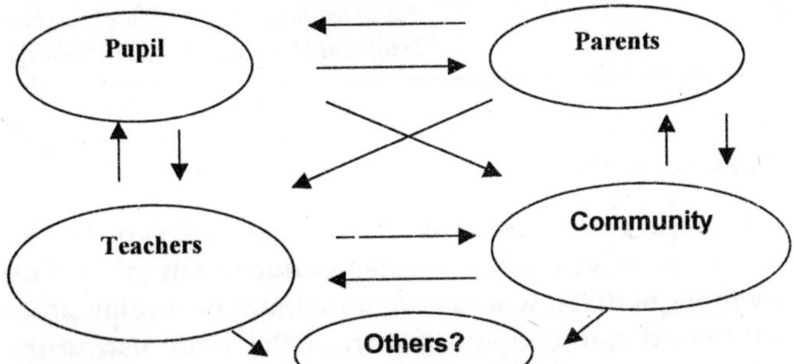

Group work may be organized in the class on how positive relationship among teachers, children, parents and members of the community may be encouraged.

Providing Quality Education to All Children, NCERT has under taken a project entitled "Innovative Teaching Strategies for Promoting Inclusive Education." The project covered nine different states of Rajasthan, Maharashtra, Uttar Pradesh, Himachal Pradesh, Delhi, Uttranchal, Mizoram, Orissa and Goa. Twenty districts were selected from these states, which covered around 1,500 children under control and experimental groups to study the effectiveness of innovative teaching strategies for promoting inclusive education. The coverage of sample may be seen from the following table:

Schools and Number of Children from Different States Covered Under the Study

States	*Dists.*	*No. of schools*	*No. of children Exp.*	*No. of children control*	*Total*	*Grand total*
9	20	36	855	641	1496	1496

Teaching Strategies Under Study

Certain teaching strategies like cooperative teaching strategies, peer tutoring and child-to-child approach were found to be useful and successful teaching strategies to address the diversity in the classroom. Effectiveness of these teaching strategies for inclusive schooling was to be studied in this particular project.

Number of Teachers and Teacher Educators Trained Under the Study

States	*Districts*	*No. of teachers trained at Hqr.*	*No. of Teachers trained at school level*
9	20	27	45

Outcome of the Study

It was found that teachers showed initial reservations about the use of cooperative teaching strategies due to a number of reasons. They thought that it would be a more time consuming procedure. They feared non-cooperation from the administrators, head teachers, and other co-teachers in the school as well as resistance from peers and parents etc. But after working with the strategies, they found that their workload was quite lighter as they were getting co-operation from peer group, older children in the school, co-teachers, parents as well as members of the community who were providing support. It was revealed from the study that children were becoming more responsible for their own learning. They were learning better. They were more involved in their work and working cooperatively with their peers. This may be viewed from the following table:

Teaching Strategies for Addressing Diversity N = 41

Sl. No.	*Teaching Strategies*	*No. of responses*	*%*
1.	Play way method	14	34
2.	Co-operating learning	28	68
3.	Peer tutoring	7	17
4.	Small Group Work	9	23
5.	IEP	7	17

(Contd.)

Sl. No.	*Teaching Strategies*	*No. of responses*	*%*
6.	Special teaching learning material/ Teaching aids (includes chart, picture, flash cards, map)	21	51
7.	Child to child approach	6	15
8.	Parents involvement	2	5
9.	Through creative activities	4	10

It may be analyzed from the above table that 68 per cent of the teachers were of the opinion that cooperative teaching strategies are the best for meeting individual needs of children in the classroom. Use of cooperative teaching strategies facilitated self-learning methods, children's involvement in the task assigned to them. It made them responsible for their own learning as well as for the learning of their peers. Fifty one per cent of the teachers were of the opinion that the use of special teaching learning material like use of charts, pictures, flash cards, maps etc., is another strategy, which can be used to enhance the performance of special need children. Play-way methods were found equally useful. Peer tutoring is found successful in language teaching. Child to child approach (15%) and small group work (23%) enhance self-confidence through participation.

A number of different methods and combinations of these methods like praising children's efforts, providing varied materials and talking to individuals were also found to be useful for addressing individual needs of children in the classroom.

Conclusion

Inclusion is bound to happen if these teaching strategies are implemented by the teachers in the classroom. Teachers and Teacher Educators need to be trained in using these successful Teaching Strategies and it has to be made an integral part of the existing general education system both at pre-service as well as at in- service level at the Elementary as well as the secondary stage. It is about bringing a change in our thinking and attitude about children with special needs and about their education. Teacher Education is to be restructured in the light of the Policy on Inclusion.

5

Education for All—Existing Realities and Challenges in Asia

Dr. Anupam Ahuja

"We are guilty of many crimes, but our worst sin is abandoning the child: neglecting the foundation of life. Many of the things we need can wait: ***the child cannot.*** We cannot answer Tomorrow. ***Her name is TODAY."***

– *Gabriela Mistral*

Setting the Scene

A presentation was made during a seminar on Inclusion at the Central Institute of Education, Delhi University. The talk mainly emphasised on the need to focus on all children, including those belonging to the marginalized groups and making collective efforts in order to achieve the EFA goal.

In the beginning the presenter shared with the group a caption she saw written on the school gate in Laos PDR. It read *All for the children, for all the children."* The words appeared to be stating the essence of the school policy in a nutshell. *The school in principle welcomed all learners and collectively worked towards meeting their needs.* The participants shared their opinion on the caption and voiced their concern about many groups of children who still need to be brought into the fold of good quality education.

The sharing of thoughts lead to the following messages getting flagged for further discussion:

- Respecting the Right of every child to quality education.
- Inclusive education a versatile tool to achieve EFA.

- Celebrating differences.
- Welcoming all learners.
- Improving teaching and learning processes for accommodating diverse needs of children.

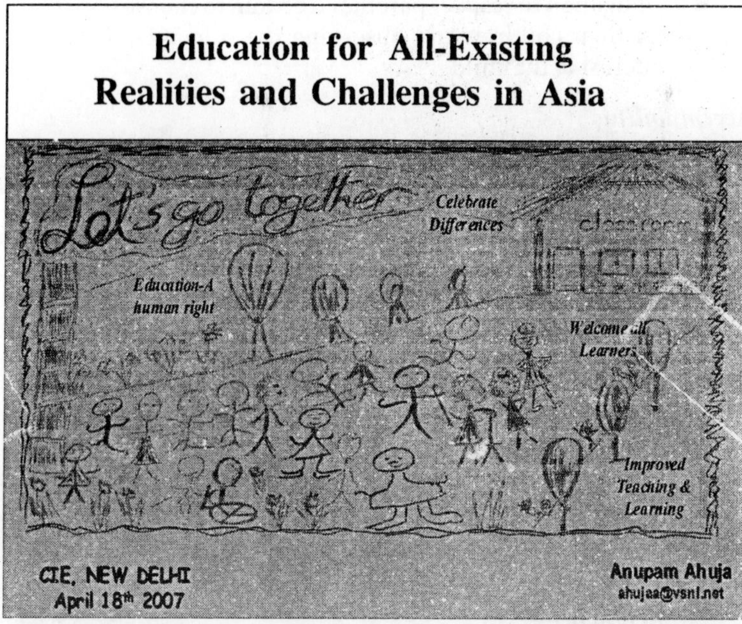

The Right to Education: A Basic Human Right for All

The presenter emphasised that the Right to Education for all children is established and confirmed in many United Nations and other international, regional and national human rights documents – including the International Covenant on Economic, Social and Cultural Rights (Article 14) and the Convention on the Rights of the Child (Articles 28 and 29). The World Declaration on Education for All and the Dakar Framework for Action as well as the Millennium Development Goals have strongly confirmed and expanded on these rights. Yet the right of many children including a large number of young girls are not being recognised.

Continuing with the discussion on the need to focus on the rights it was stated that these relate to availability of quality education, acceptability, accessibility and adaptability:

Availability

- Obligation to ensure free compulsory education for all children in the country up to at least the minimum age of employment.
- Obligation to respect parental freedom to choose education for their children and observing the principle of the best interest of the child.

Acceptability

- Obligation to set minimum standards of quality for education, including the contents in textbooks and curricula, methods of teaching, school discipline, health and safety and professional requirements for teachers.
- Obligation to improve the quality of education by ensuring that the entire education system conforms to all human rights.

Accessibility

- Obligation to eliminate exclusion from education based on internationally prohibited grounds of discrimination (race, colour, sex, language, religion, opinion, origin of birth, social or economic status, HIV/AIDS status and disability).
- Obligation to eliminate gender and racial discrimination in education by ensuring equal enjoyment of all human rights in practice.

Adaptability

- Obligation to design and implement education for children excluded from schooling (e.g. refugees or internally displaced children, street or working children).
- Obligations to adapt education to the best interests of each child, especially regarding children with special needs and minority or indigenous children.
- Obligation to apply indivisibility of human rights as guidance so as to advance all human rights through education.

The group agreed that providing quality education to say the children with disabilities is not a matter of pitying their condition and making " some random provisions" but a matter of recognizing their legitimate rights.

Purpose of Schooling

This discussion was followed by a deliberation on the purpose of schooling. A fable written by George Reavis (Appendix 1) was shared. This story highlighted the need to focus on each learner's strength and not to force children to follow a rigid curriculum. The participants expressed their opinion and shared their diverse views on what they felt was the moral of the story.

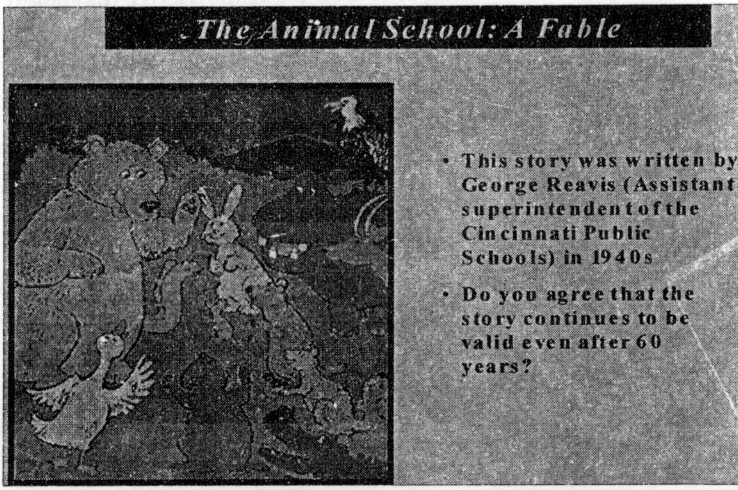

This was followed by sharing some other concerns as regards the intentions and purpose of schooling in both formal and informal settings. The presenter shared her own perspective on the purpose of schooling and stated that any school setting ought:

- To be safe and secure
- To develop a sense of self
- To be able to make choices
- To be able to communicate
- To be part of community
- To be able to live in a changing world
- To be prepared for the many transitions of life
- To be able to make contributions that are valued.

A rich discussion followed and each participant was given time to reflect on their own perceptions regarding the purpose of schooling.

Catering to Diversity

The need for planning learning appropriately considering the varied needs of children in the class was emphasised. Though children learn from their families, from contact with parents and friends and by participating in diverse activities yet we send them to school. Considering this given reality the group pondered over the question; 'Why should children attend school? They felt that attending school can help to promote learning provided we acknowledge that before coming to school children know a lot and attempts are made to link this learning with school learning. These discussions lead to considering factors responsible for exclusion from school. It was unanimously agreed that exclusion clearly has a social, financial, ethnic and lingual base.

An interesting discussion on the following issues followed:

- What are the forms of education currently available for the marginalized groups?
- How far does or planning include the excluded children?
- Do we respect childrens' right to choose a type of education (special, integrated or inclusive)?
- How far are we prepared to think out of the special education box?
- Is planning special school settings for children with disabilities also not a form of exclusive thinking?
- Is "special needs" not another demeaning label?
- How can we extend the meaning and scope of special needs?
- Who are the children who feel excluded even when inside the classroom?

Understanding Inclusive Practice

A rich discussion followed on the difference between special education, integrated education and inclusive education; the three different forms of school settings that exist for marginalized groups.

The discussion raised the need to focus on the following excluded groups of children in inclusive settings;

- Physically and intellectually challenged children.
- Girls and boys who should be in school but are not (e.g. children who work at home, in the fields or who have paying jobs to help their families survive).

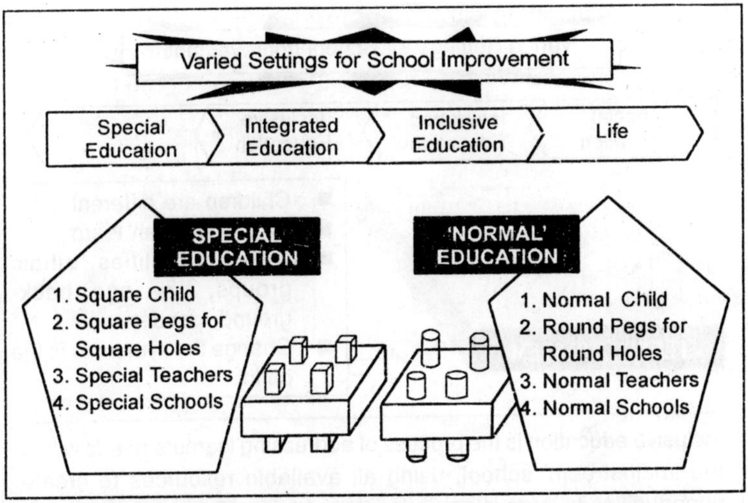

Source: Stubbs, S. (2002), Inclusive Education: Where there are few resources; The all as Alliance, in cooperation with NAD Indonesian Context.

Source: Implementation of IE in Indoesia – A persons Disabilities perspective; A presentation material by Didi Tarsidi.

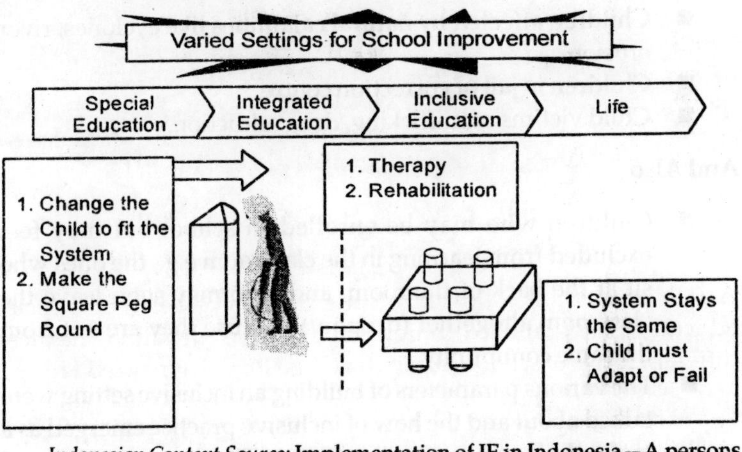

Indonesian Context Source: Implementation of IE in Indonesia – A persons Disabilities Perspective; A presentation material by Didi Tarsidi.

- Children in living in poverty/slums.
- Children belonging to ethnic, linguistic and religious minorities.
- Children affected by hunger, malnourishment, HIV etc.
- Abused children.

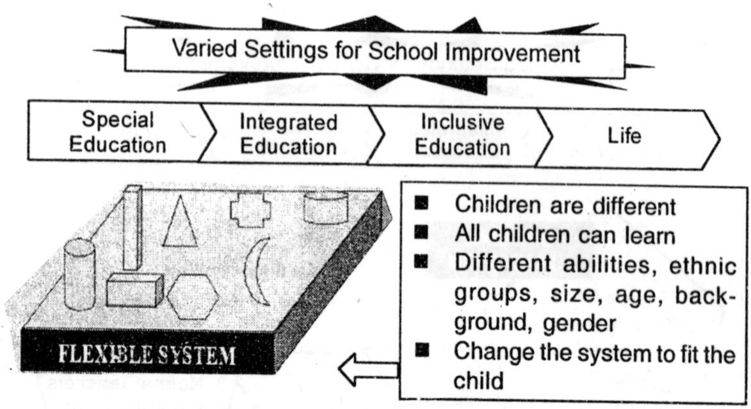

Inclusive education is the process of addressing learners needs within the 'mainstream' school, using all available resources to create opportunities to learn in preparing them for life. **The emphasis is on reviewing schools and systems and changing them rather than trying to change students.**

- Children affected by natural calamities like cyclones, river erosion.
- Children in jail or correction centre.
- Child victims of trafficking, drug addiction.

And Also

- Children who may be enrolled in school but may feel excluded from learning in the classroom e.g., the ones who sit at the back of the room, and who may soon leave the classroom altogether (dropout) because they are not from the same community.
- The various parameters of building an inclusive setting were talked about and the how of inclusive practice emerged as a major challenge for the practioners. The discussion focused on how an inclusive school is for every child and on the need to look beyond children with disabilities while encouraging inclusive practice. Further elaborations flagged the issue that implementing the Rights of the Child (CRC) can never be limited to only one group and inclusive classrooms promote:

- Team teaching
- Peer-teaching
- Positive groupings
- Problem oriented teaching
- Open and flexible curricula
- Individualised Education
- Providing support when needed.

The discussion lead to delineating collectively ways of promoting inclusive practice in varied classroom settings in the country.

To help the group further understand the reasons for promoting inclusive practice the presenter shared the educational, social, economic justification of inclusive practice.

Educational Justification

While educating all children together we develop ways of teaching, which respond to individual differences and therefore, benefit all children.

Social Justification

- Change attitudes to differences by educating all children together.
- Forms the basis of a society, which encourages people to live together in peace.
- Human differences are natural, contribute to the richness of every society, and must, of course, be reflected in schools.

Economic Justification

It is likely to be less costly to establish and maintain schools, which educate all children together than to set-up a complex system of different types of schools specializing in the education of specific groups of children.

The group agreed that as a result of the World Education Forum in Dakar, 2000 the challenge of exclusion from education has been put on the political agenda in many countries. This has helped to focus attention on a much broader range of children who may be excluded from or marginalized within education systems because of their apparent difficulties. These may include:

- Those who are enrolled in education but are excluded from learning.
- Those who are not enrolled in schools but who could participate if schools were more flexible in their responses and welcoming in their approach.
- The relatively small group of children with more severe impairments who may have a need for some form of additional support.

The Dakar World Education Forum recognized the urgency to address the needs of all learners.

"...Education systems must be inclusive, actively seeking out children who are not enrolled, and responding flexibly to the circumstances and needs of all learners..."

Inclusive Environment in the Classroom
Needs to be Planned with Care

The discussion led the group to agree that the ultimate goal of inclusive education is a school where all are participating and treated equally. However, it is important to remember that inclusive education is a constant process to ensure that Education for All really is for *all*. When looking to reach the students who do not participate fully, it is important the group was told to give attention to the forms of education provided for all children. A consideration needs to be given to the existing opportunity to participate in school and on both the children who are excluded and the reasons thereof. Care has to be taken when looking into the picture of which children come to be categorized as being in some way "special" or "excluded" within particular contexts.

In communities where all children, including children with disabilities, are sent to the local schools, the community and the school need to take responsibility for *all* children. Bringing special needs thinking, where one group of children is identified as different, into such a context might diminish this sense of responsibility. It is also important to remember that a child categorized in one context as "special" might not be so in another and that children categorized within one "group" might have more different than similar needs. Drawing from the experiences from different countries the presenter mentioned that it is not sufficient to only look at how to integrate one particular group of children, such as children with disabilities.

The participants agreed that in some schools one can see that children categorized as having special needs might be in the same classroom, but have separate tasks to do or even a separate teacher. Communication and interaction with the other pupils then become difficult, and eventually the child is excluded *within* the class. Integrating one group of students may not address other grounds for discrimination in classrooms. So, when moving towards more inclusive policies and practice, the focus needs to be on strategies to remove barriers to learning and participation for *all* children.

It is necessary to look into how schools can be modified or changed to make sure that the education is relevant to the local context, includes and treats all pupils with respect and is flexible so that all can participate. This requires re-directing resources and inter-sectorial cooperation and has implications on the following areas:

Policy Development

In some countries policies exist that open up a possibility for authorities not to take responsibility for certain groups of children. Often this applies to children with severe intellectual disability, but it might also refer, for instance, to ethnic minorities or children without a birth certificate. Also in a great number of countries, the education of some specific groups of learners might be the responsibility of another authority than the Ministry of Education. Often this allows for a situation where these learners are not expected or encouraged to participate in mainstream education.

Curriculum Development

Within the education system the curriculum may be one of the major obstacles for inclusion. In many countries the curriculum is extensive and demanding, and centrally designed and rigid. The curriculum can facilitate the development of more inclusive settings if it leaves for the school or teacher to make adaptations so that it makes sense in the local context and for the individual learner. Linked to this is the issue of language of instruction. In many countries it may be different than the language that students use at home making it difficult for some of them to follow what is happening in the classroom. Bilingual education can help to address this problem.

Teacher Training

Often much of the teaching in the classroom is based on rote learning, meticulous following of textbooks and copying. In order to change the practices in the classroom into more child-friendly and flexible practices, teachers and schools need training building on the existing expertise. There also needs to be a school environment that encourages risk-taking so teachers have the time and dare try out new approaches, and for example do not have to worry about inspectors or head teachers not liking what they are doing. A whole school approach to school improvement has proven more effective in establishing change in schools, than training a few of the staff.

Local Capacity Building and Community Involvement

The first task in building effective support for schools is to mobilize the resources that already exist in schools and the local community. In addition there might be need for some external support such as teams of teacher trainers or support teachers coming in on a regular basis. For instance, in some countries, the roles of the inspectors have changed from "grading" schools and teachers to giving pedagogical support on a regular basis. Often this type of support can also be derived from the elders in the local community.

Why Promote Inclusive Education?

The discussion also focused on how to plan "Schools for all" including children with disabilities and young people. The participants agreed on the following reasons as to why we need to promote inclusive education:

- It acknowledges that all children can learn.
- It enables education structures, systems and methodologies to meet the needs of all children.
- It can contribute to the quality of education for all.
- It enables children with disabilities to stay with families and communities.
- It is part of a wider strategy to promote an inclusive society
- It is consistent with the key principles of the CRC.

In inclusive education the system has to change and not the child. A twin track approach to inclusive education is necessary.

Change Education Systems

Pay Attention to the Specific Needs of Individual Children

School improvement may be a result of inclusive education, or it may provide the opportunity for more inclusive practices to be promoted. Whichever route is taken, school improvement must take place.

In the final part of the talk the speaker shared the following workable ways that indicates we can support inclusive education:

- Carry out situational analyses.
- Develop pilot schools.
- Lobby for system change in education.
- Promote inclusive policies and legislation.
- Find simple and cost effective ways of overcoming barriers in the physical environment.
- Create child friendly learning environments.
- Use simple, clear and consistent language.
- Make learning enjoyable.
- Make education more relevant to daily life and home situations.
- Accept that children learn at different rates and vary teaching methods accordingly.

- Respond flexibly and creatively to the individual needs of children.
- Be flexible about seating arrangements – use mats, pebbles, old tyres etc. as teaching material.
- Use multi-sensory teaching methods that attend to the diversity of senses.
- Promote active learning and child to child activities.
- Encourage teachers to observe each other and problem solve together.
- Involve parents and community members in education.

The focus of the work the participants agreed needs to be on:

- Strengthening inclusive approaches in the National EFA plans, education policies and strategies.
- Developing approaches and resource materials to address diverse needs in education.
- Supporting national capacity building for government policy-making and system management.
- Gathering and disseminating information and ideas.

The session ended with the presenter cautioning the participants to remember that:

- Inclusion is not a utopian dream, which leads to inclusive societies overnight.
- Conflicting views, contradictions, inequality will perhaps stay.
- The challenge is to work collectively and find contextual options to address exclusion.

Finally, she thanked the participants for listening to the thoughts presented and participating actively and sharing their view-points.

APPENDIX 1

The Animal School: A Fable

By George Reavis

Once upon a time the animals decided they must do something heroic to meet the problems of a "new world" so they organized a school. They had adopted an **activity curriculum** consisting of **running, climbing, swimming and flying.** To make it easier to administer the curriculum, all the animals took all the subjects.

The **duck** was excellent in swimming. In fact, better than his instructor. But he made only passing grades in flying and was very poor in running. Since he was slow in running, he had to stay after school and also drop swimming in order to practice running. This was kept up until his webbed feet were badly worn and he was only average in swimming. But average was acceptable in school so nobody worried about that, except the duck.

The **rabbit** started at the top of the class in running but had a nervous breakdown because of so much make-up work in swimming.

The **squirrel** was excellent in climbing until he developed frustration in the flying class where his teacher made him start from the ground up instead of the treetop down. He also developed a "charlie horse" from overexertion and then got a C in climbing and D in running.

The **eagle** was a problem child and was disciplined severely. In the climbing class, he beat all the others to the top of the tree but insisted on using his own way to get there.

At the end of the year, an **abnormal eel** that could swim exceeding well and also run, climb and fly a little had the highest average and was valedictorian.

The **prairie dogs** stayed out of school *and fought the tax levy* because the administration would not add digging and burrowing to the curriculum. They apprenticed their children to a badger and later joined the groundhogs and gophers to start a successful private school.

Does this fable have a moral?

PART–II
Possibilities and Challenges

6

समावेशन (Inclusion) से जुड़े कुछ मुद्दे

डॉ० ऊषा शर्मा

राधिका दिल्ली के प्राथमिक नगर निगम विद्यालय, संगम विहार की तीसरी कक्षा की छात्रा है। वह बातचीत करने में बेहद कुशल और अपने कक्षा-कार्य को बहुत सलीके से करने में दक्ष है। सबके साथ बहुत अच्छे ढ़ग से व्यवहार करती है। लेकिन खेल के मैदान में गुमसुम-सी एक तरफ़ बैठी रहती है। उस समय उसके चेहरे की बदलती रंगतें और रेखाएँ उसके दिल का हाल बयान कर देती हैं। क्या आप बता सकते हैं—उसकी उदासी का कारण?

मोहित दिल्ली के सरकारी विद्यालय तुगलकाबाद में कक्षा पाँच का छात्र है। वह कक्षा-कार्य करने में बेहद सुस्त है। आँखे मिचका-मिचकाकर ब्लैकबोर्ड की तरफ़ देखता है। कई बार आँखों को मलता है। उसके शिक्षक उसकी इन हरकतों से खासे 'परेशान' हैं। वह लगभग रोज़ डाँट खाता है और भरी कक्षा में अपमानित होता है। लेकिन अपने संगी-साथियों में कथा बाँचने में एकदम 'परफ़ेक्ट' है। मौखिक गणित (मेंटल मैथ्स) में अव्वल नंबर पर रहता है। लेकिन ब्लैकबोर्ड में देखकर कार्य करने में उसकी धीमी गति और कक्षा की अन्य गतिविधियों में उसका असहज व्यवहार का परिणाम है—उसके कपोलों पर लुढ़कते मोटे-मोटे आँसू जो उसकी व्यथा कह डालते हैं। क्या आप समझ पाएगे उसकी व्यथा?

सोनम रोज़ ज़िद करती है कि वह स्कूल जाएगी, लेकिन स्कूल वाले उसे दाखिला नहीं देते। कारण-सोनम मंदबुद्धि बालिका है। उसे इस तरह सामान्य विद्यार्थियों के साथ सामान्य विद्यालय में नहीं पढ़ाया जा सकता। जबकि वास्तविकता यह है कि सोनम प्रशिक्षण योग्य मंदबुद्धि बालिका है।

उसके माता-पिता उसे विशेष विद्यालय, जो कि उसके घर से लगभग 14 किलोमीटर दूर है, में भेजने में असमर्थ हैं। सोनम क्या करे? क्या शिक्षा से वंचित रखा जाए?

उपर्युक्त तीनों दृष्टांतों का पढ़ते समय संभवतः आपकी आँखों के सामने राधिका, मोहित और सोनम का एक रेखाचित्र-सा खिंच गया होगा। इतना ही नहीं आप उनके विद्यालय, परिवेश और अन्य गतिविधियों के बारे में कल्पना की उड़ान भरने लगे होंगे। उनके प्रति अपार करूणा, दया, सहानुभूति का भाव भी उमड़ने लगा होगा। इन तीनों स्थितियों में एक सामाजिक व्यक्ति, शिक्षक, अभिभावक, प्रधानाचार्य के रूप में आप अपनी क्या भूमिका तय करेंगे?

संविधान के 86वें संशोधन में शिक्षा को एक मौलिक अधिकार का दर्जा दिया गया, जिसके परिणामस्वरूप शिक्षा प्राप्त करना प्रत्येक बच्चे का अधिकार बन गया। स्थिति यह बन गई हैं कि अब कोई भी विद्यालय जाति, धर्म, लिंग, अक्षमता के आधार पर बच्चे को विद्यालय में दाखिला लेने से वंचित नहीं कर सकता। धीरे-धीरे यह चिंतन भी विकसित होने लगा कि 'अशक्तता' के नाम पर बच्चे को सामान्य विद्यालय की मुख्यधारा से वंचित नहीं रखा जाना चाहिए। राष्ट्रीय पाठ्यचर्या की रूपरेखा (2005) में स्पष्टतः कहा गया है कि 'पृथक्करण या अलगाव' न तो विकलांग विद्यार्थियों के लिए अच्छा है और न ही सामान्य विद्यार्थियों के लिए। सामाजिक आवश्यकता यह है कि विद्यार्थियों को अन्य दूसरे विद्यार्थियों के साथ समावेशी (इन्क्लूसिव) स्कूलों में पढ़ाया जाना चाहिए। ये स्कूल प्रभावपूर्ण एवं सशक्त शिक्षा-शास्त्रीय व्यवहार वाले होते हैं। समावेशी शिक्षा की आवश्यकता इस बात से जाहिर है कि आई० ई० डी० सी० योजना के अंतर्गत विशेष आवश्यकता वाले शिक्षार्थियों के लिए 100 प्रतिशत वित्तीय प्रावधान होने के बावजूद भी इन शिक्षार्थियों की संख्या का मात्र 1-2 प्रतिशत ही वास्तव में सामान्य स्कूलों से जुड़ सका। एकीकरण की धीमी गति के कारण उत्पन्न असंतोष, इसमें लगने वाली लागत व अन्य लोगों द्वारा विद्यार्थियों को सहजता से लेने में इन्क्लूसिव वातावरण के लाभ ने एक बुनियादी परिवर्तन की माँग को जन्म दिया। अंतर्राष्ट्रीय और राष्ट्रीय स्तर पर इसके पुनः अवधारणीकरण ने इन्क्लूसिव शिक्षा की ओर मार्ग प्रशस्त किया।

समावेशी शिक्षा (इन्क्लूसिव एजुकेशन) के बारे में आगे और गहन रूप से चर्चा करने से पहले इसकी स्पष्ट अवधारणा से परिचित होना आवश्यक है।

मानव संसाधन विकास मंत्रालय के अनुसार, 'समावेशी' का अर्थ है–सभी सीखने वाले, युवा–चाहे अशक्त हों या नहीं, साधारण विद्यालय-पूर्व व्यवस्था, विद्यालयों और सामुदायिक शिक्षा केंद्रों में उपयुक्त सहयोगी सेवाओं के साथ आपस में मिल–जुलकर सीखने में समर्थ हों। समावेश का अर्थ है–मुख्यधारा के विद्यालयों में विशेष आवश्यकता वाले बच्चों का उनके अन्य सहपाठियों के साथ शिक्षा प्रदान करने की प्रक्रिया। निश्चित तौर पर यह प्रक्रिया जटिल अवश्य है लेकिन असंभव नहीं। इस प्रक्रिया की जटिलता का प्रमुख कारण है–वैभिन्नय को समेटना, सहेजना और पोषित करना।

'समावेशन' की संकल्पना, महत्त्व अथवा जरूरत को स्पष्ट करते हुए राष्ट्रीय पाठ्यचर्या की रूपरेखा 2005 में यह कहा गया है कि 'समोवशन की नीति' को हर स्कूल और सारी शिक्षा व्यवस्था में व्यापक रूप से लागू किए जाने की जरूरत है। बच्चे के जीवन के हर क्षेत्र में, वह चाहे स्कूल में हो या बाहर, सभी बच्चों की भागीदारी सुनिश्चित किए जाने की जरूरत है। स्कूलों को ऐसे केन्द्रों में बनाए जाने की आवश्यकता है, जहाँ बच्चों को जीवन की तैयारी कराई जाए और यह सुनिश्चित किया जाए की सभी बच्चों, खासकर शारीरिक या मानसिक रूप से असमर्थ बच्चों, समाज के हाशिए पर जीने वाले बच्चों और कठिन परिस्थितियों में जीने वाले बच्चों को शिक्षा के इस महत्वपूर्ण क्षेत्र के सबसे ज्यादा फ़ायदे मिले। अपनी प्रतिभा का प्रर्दशन करने के मौके और सहपाठियों के साथ बाँटने के मौके देना बच्चों में प्रोत्साहन और जुड़ाव को पोषण देने के शक्तिशाली तरीके हैं। बच्चों को शुरू में ही संकीर्ण संज्ञानात्मक आधार पर वर्गीकृत करके स्कूल उस विविधता को भी क्षति पहुँचाते हैं जो बच्चों की क्षमताओं और प्रतिभाओं में होती है। प्रत्येक बच्चे के साथ व्यक्तिगत स्तर पर जुड़ने की बजाए बच्चों को अपने प्रारम्भिक जीवन में ही संज्ञानात्मक पदों पर रख दिया जाता है। श्रेष्ठतम विद्यार्थी, सामान्य से कम स्तर के और असफल, अधिकतर मामलों में बच्चों के पास अपने पद से खुद हटने के मौके नहीं होते। ठप्पा लगाने की इस भयावह प्रक्रिया का बच्चों पर बहुत ही विनाशकारी प्रभाव पड़ता है। स्कूल बेतुकी हद तक जाकर बच्चों से इन ठप्पों को आत्मसात करवाते हैं। स्कूल कुछ बच्चों को मंदबुद्धि कहते हैं, यहाँ तक कि उन्हें बिठाते भी अलग हैं और ऐसे सूचक कक्षा में लगा देते हैं जिससे बच्चों का विभाजन बहुत स्पष्ट रूप से दिखने लगता है। सही उत्तर पता न होने का भय कई बच्चों को कक्षा

में बिल्कुल मौन रखता है जिससे वह भागीदारी और सीखने के समान अवसरों से वंचित रह जाते हैं।

उपर्युक्त चर्चा से इतना तो स्पष्ट है कि प्रत्येक बच्चे की अपनी कुछ विशिष्ट विशेषताएँ व आवश्यकताएँ होती हैं। उनकी विशिष्ट आवश्यकताओं के कारण उन्हें किन्हीं 'विशिष्ट ठप्पों से सुसज्जित' करने की मानसिकता और प्रक्रिया निश्चित तौर पर अनुचित प्रतीत होती है। बल्कि कोशिश ऐसी होनी चाहिए कि सभी बच्चों की जरूरतों की पहचान की जाए और उन्हें पूरा करने की ईमानदारी से कोशिश की जाए। बहरहाल, इस समावेशी शिक्षा से जुड़े कुछ बुनियादी मुद्दे और भी हैं, जैसे–

- शिक्षा प्रत्येक बच्चों का मौलिक अधिकार है और उसे यह अवसर दिया जाना चाहिए कि वह सीखने के अपेक्षित स्तर को प्राप्त कर सके और उसे बनाए रख सके।
- शिक्षा-व्यवस्था को इस प्रकार संरचित किया जाए और शैक्षिक कार्यक्रमों को इस प्रकार क्रियान्वित किया जाए, जिससे बच्चों की विशेषताओं और लक्षणों के वैभिन्नत को ध्यान में रखा जा सकें।
- विशेष आवश्यकता वाले बच्चों की पहुँच सामान्य विद्यालयों तक अवश्य होनी चाहिए और उनकी आवश्यकताओं को पूरा करने के लिए शिक्षार्थी केंद्रित शिक्षा-शास्त्र पर बल दिया जाना चाहिए।

उपर्युक्त बिंदुओं पर गौर किया जाए तो संपूर्ण शिक्षा-व्यवस्था को पुनः संरचित करने की आवश्यकता प्रतीत होती है। समावेशी शिक्षा को प्रभावी बनाने के लिए, उसके साथ न्याय करने के लिए न केवल प्रतिबद्धता की आवश्यकता है, बल्कि निष्ठा, ईमानदारी और स्वीकृति-भाव वाले दृष्टिकोण की भी आवश्यकता है। यदि इन बिंदुओं को शिक्षा से जुड़े विभिन्न संदर्भों में परखा जाए तो कई और प्रश्न उठ खडे होते हैं–

- क्या विद्यालय सभी बच्चों को दाखिला देते हैं या किसी कसौटी के आधार पर दाखिला अस्वीकृत कर देते हैं?
- क्या विद्यालय के पास उन संसाधनों का कोई प्रावधान है जो प्रत्येक बच्चे की बुद्धि और विकास के लिए जरूरी है?
- क्या विद्यालयी शिक्षकों में वह कुशलता है कि वे विविध क्षमताओं, आवश्यकताओं वाले बच्चों को एक साथ पढ़ा सकें और क्या वे सभी को पढ़ाने के लिए एक ही विधि का प्रयोग करते हैं?

- क्या शिक्षा और अधिकारीगण विशेष शैक्षिक आवश्यकता वाले बच्चों का स्वागत करते हैं या उन्हें एक बोझ समझते हैं?
- क्या कक्षा में विशेष शैक्षिक आवश्यकता वाले बच्चों को अलग-अलग रखा जाता है या कक्षा-कक्ष की गतिविधियों में संपूर्ण भागीदारिता निभाने का अवसर दिया जाता है?
- क्या अभिभावक विद्यार्थी की प्रगति में बराबर के साझेदार हैं या शिक्षक उन्हें विद्यालय के अहम् हिस्से के रूप में स्वीकार नहीं करते?
- क्या शिक्षक यह महसूस करते हैं कि सभी विद्यार्थियों में कुछ विशेषताएँ होती हैं और क्या वे प्रत्यक्ष वैयक्तिक अनुदेशन की महत्ता से परिचित हैं या वे व्याख्यान अथवा 'पूरी कक्षा के लिए एक तरीका' वाले उपागम को प्राथमिकता देते हैं?
- क्या विद्यालय कक्षा, विद्यालय से बाहर अशक्तता और बिना अशक्तता वाले विद्यार्थियों में परस्पर संवाद, अंत: क्रिया को बढ़ावा देता है?
- क्या केवल शैक्षणिक कौशलों पर ही ध्यान दिया जाता है अथवा सामाजिक कौशलों को भी महत्व दिया जाता है?
- क्या विद्यालय, जहाँ तक संभव हो, समान परीक्षण और मूल्यांकन अनुभवों में सभी विद्यार्थियों को शामिल करता है या कुछ को अनुभवों की उस दुनिया से बाहर कर देता है—वैकल्पिक मूल्यांकन प्रक्रियाओं के बारे में चिंतन के बिना और इस विश्वास के साथ कि इन अनुभवों से उन विद्यार्थियों को कोई लाभ नहीं मिलेगा?
- क्या शिक्षकों ने विभिन्न विद्यार्थियों के लिए वैकल्पिक लक्ष्य और अपेक्षाएँ निर्मित की हैं अथवा सभी के लिए समान लक्ष्य रखे/हैं।
- क्या विद्यालयकर्मी विभिन्न समस्याओं को सुलझाने के लिए एक-दूसरे के साथ, विशेष शिक्षक, विशेष विद्यालय के साथ सहयोगात्मक रवैया अपनाते हैं?

इन प्रश्नों पर गहन दृष्टि से चिंतन किए जाने की आवश्यकता, है। वस्तुत: 'समावेशी शिक्षा' की संकल्पना को 'काग़ज' से 'जमीन' पर उतारने के लिए शिक्षा के मुख्यत: दो स्तरों पर बुनियादी परिवर्तन की जरूरत है—सेवा-पूर्व अध्यापक-शिक्षा और सेवाकालीन अध्यापक-शिक्षा। जहाँ तक सेवा-पूर्व अध्यापक शिक्षा का सवाल है—समावेशी शिक्षा को एक अनिवार्य विषय के रूप में स्थान दिया जाना चाहिए। जिससे आधारभूत संकल्पना, उपागम और प्रविधियों को

गहराई के साथ समझा–परखा जा सके। अब रहा सेवाकालीन अध्यापक–शिक्षा का सवाल–समावेशी शिक्षा को सभी स्तरों (प्राथमिक, टी० जी० टी०, पी० जी० टी०) पर आयोजित होने वाले अंत: सेवा प्रशिक्षण कार्यक्रम के पाठ्यक्रम की रूपरेखा में उचित स्थान दिया जाना चाहिए। जिससे शिक्षकों के साथ संवाद करते हुए जमीनी वास्तविकताओं, समस्याओं से अवगत करते हुए उनके व्यवहारिक समाधान सुझाए जा सकें।

राज्य शैक्षिक अनुसंधान एवं प्रशिक्षण परिषद् तथा विभिन्न मंडलीय शिक्षा एवं शिक्षण संस्थानों (दिल्ली में स्थित) इस दिशा में उचित कदम उठाए हैं। जहाँ एक और शिक्षक–प्रशिक्षणार्थियों के लिए समावेशी शिक्षा पर आधारित विभिन्न कार्यशालाओं का आयोजन किया गया वहीं दूसरी ओर अंत: सेवा–प्रशिक्षण कार्यक्रमों का आयोजन करते हुए सेवारत शिक्षको को समावेशी शिक्षा से परिचित कराया गया। हालाँकि समावेशी शिक्षा की दिशा में ये प्रयास सराहनीय हैं। लेकिन अपने बृहत् संदर्भो में ये प्रयास नाकाफ़ी हैं। अभी इस दिशा में और अधिक चिंतन, कर्मशीलता की जरूरत है।

कार्यक्रमों के दौरान मिलीं प्रतिक्रियाओं का स्वरूप मिश्र–स्वरूपी था, यथा–

- यह सब करना बहुत मुश्किल है, क्योंकि स्कूल में इतना समय नहीं मिलता कि इन बच्चों के लिए कुछ अतिरिक्त कार्य किया जाए सामग्री जुटाई जाए।
- अनेक बार एक कक्षा में 60–70 बच्चे होते हैं उनकी जरूरतों को पूरा कर पाना मुश्किल हो जाता है, फिर इन अशक्त बच्चों को कैसे सँभाला जायेगा?
- भीड़ भरी कक्षाओं में बच्चों को सँभालना कठिन है, ठीक तरह से पढ़ाना तो दूर की बात है।
- सरकार जो सेवाएँ उपलब्ध कराती है, उसे कभी समय पर मुहैया नहीं कराती।
- अशक्त बच्चों की सही–सही पहचान की उतनी प्रगाढ़ समझ़ नहीं बन पाई है।
- यह एक अच्छा प्रयास है, ऐसे अशक्त बच्चों को पढ़ाना उनकी क्षमताओं को विकसित करना हमारा ही दायित्व है।
- मेरा बच्चा भी मंद बुद्धि है। जब उसे पब्लिक स्कूल वालों ने लेने से

मना कर दिया तो मुझे बहुत दुख हुआ था, अब कम से कम मैं उनके विरूद्ध आवाज तो उठा सकती हूँ।

- ऐसे कार्यक्रमों की अवधि एक दिन न होकर पाँच-दस दिन होनी चाहिए, जिससे हमें सभी चीजों को समझने का अवसर मिल सके।
- लो मैडम, आप ने तो हमारा एक काम और बढ़ा दिया। हमारे पास वैसे ही स्कूल के चार्ज कम थे--अब यह भी हमें करना होगा। इसके लिए तो हर स्कूल में एक विशेष शिक्षक की नियुक्ति होनी चाहिए।
- हमें आज कई बातों का खुलासा मिला है। हम तो समझते थे, बच्चे पढ़ाई पर ध्यान नहीं देते, ढीट हैं, कम समझ वाले हैं, लेकिन अब पता चला कि वे स्वयं कितनी तकलीफों, समस्याओं से जूझ रहे हैं।
- यह बताओ कि स्कूल में बिजली, पानी, शौचालय की व्यवस्था हैं नहीं–फिर पढाएँ कैसे, सिलेबस कैसे पूरा करें?

यदि दिल्ली 'भारत की राजधानी' के सरकारी, निजी, अनुदान वाले विद्यालयों की ढाँचागत सुविधाओं पर नजर डालें तो स्थिति बहुत बेहतर नजर नहीं आती। सबसे पहले और अहम् बात कि विशेष आवश्यकता वाले विद्यार्थियों को 'सामान्य' विद्यालयों में दाखिला मिलना ही दुष्कर है और अगर दाखिला मिल भी गया तो उनकी आवश्यकताओं को पूरा करने की सुध, चाह का अभाव नज़र आता है। आइए, अब विशेष रूप से बात करते हैं–सरकारी तंत्र में 'फँसे या बसे' सरकारी विद्यालयों की। अधिकांश विद्यालयों में उचित भवन, कक्षा-कक्षों का अभाव है। कमरे कम और बच्चे ज्यादा हैं और शिक्षकों की संख्या भी कम हैं। कई विद्यालयों में तो एक सौ तेरह विद्यार्थी एक ही कक्षा में पढ़ते हैं। गर्मी में तो और भी बुरा हाल होता है। बच्चों के लिए पीने योग्य पानी का अभाव है। नल हैं–लेकिन पानी नहीं। पानी है तो टंकी खुली और गंदी है। शिक्षकों के पास 'मिनरल वाटर' की बोतलें हैं। उन्हें बच्चों की परवाह नहीं है। शौचालयों की व्यवस्था तो और भी भयावह है। लड़कों के विद्यालयों में कई बार ऐसा नज़ारा भी देखने को मिलता है कि स्कूल की चारदीवारी की रंगत और हवा में तैरती दुर्गंध बता देती है। लड़के शौचालय के लिए किस जगह का इस्तेमाल करते हैं। लड़कियों के लिए स्थिति बेहद कष्टप्रद है। वे लड़कों की तरह 'खुले' में तो जा नही सकतीं और शौचालयों में पानी नहीं है, सीवर बंद हैं। माहवारी और दस्त की हालत में कई लड़कियों को स्कूल से छुट्टी लेनी पड़ती है। अन्यथा कई बीमारियों को निमंत्रण मिल जाता है। कक्षा-कक्षों में धूल,

काग़ज, कूड़े की बहुलता अकसर यह चुगली कर जाती है कि विद्यालय में सफाई का क्या हाल है। कमरों में पंखे, बल्ब मौजूद नहीं है। अगर पंखे हैं तो पंखुडियाँ मुड़ी हुई हैं। अगर पंखे सही सलामत हैं तो बिजली आँख-मिचौनी खेलती है। जब बस नहीं चलता तो शिक्षक कमरे के बाहर कुसी डालकर बैठ जाते हैं, बच्चों का फिर कोई कुछ नहीं सोचता। ऐसा नहीं है कि दिल्ली के सभी सरकारी विद्यालयों में ऐसी स्थिति है, हाँ लेकिन अधिकांशतः विद्यालयों में यह स्थिति देखने को मिलती है। प्राथमिक विद्यालयों में पुस्तकालय एक-दो अलमारियों में बंद होकर धूल फाँकता है। एक शिक्षक-एक कक्षा की संकल्पना के चलते शिक्षकों को इतना समय नहीं मिल पाता कि वे कुछ सृजनात्मक कार्य कर सकें। ऊपर से वेतन बिल बनाना, कई तरह के चार्ज (परीक्षा, यूनीफार्म, छात्रवृत्ति, ब्यॉज फंड, पी० टी० ए० फंड आदि) का भी काम करना होता है। जबकि एक कक्षा हर रोज़, पूरे समय उन शिक्षकों के हवाले होती हैं। लेकिन अनेक शिक्षक ऐसे भी हैं जो संवदेन-शून्य हैं, हर वक्त छड़ी का हाथ में होना, चेहरे पर त्यौरियाँ होना उनके लिए आम बात है। कुछ शिक्षक कुछ सृजनात्मक कार्य करना चाहते हैं तो उनके पुराने साथी शिक्षक उन्हें लगातार हतोत्साहित करते रहते हैं। रही-सही कसर सरकारी व्यवस्था पूरी कर देती है। पाठ्यक्रम पूरा कराने का दबाब, परीक्षा-परिणाम बेहतर करने का तनाव और सक्रिय गतिविधि को 'अनुशासनहीनता' की संज्ञा देने की कसक–उस सृजनशील शिक्षक की सारी सृजनात्मकता पर प्रश्नचिह्न लगा उसे कटघरे में खड़ा कर देता है।

आइए, अब एक नजर डालते हैं–सरकारी वित्तीय प्रावधानों पर। हर विद्यालय को विद्यालय कल्याण समिति के तहत और सर्व शिक्षा अभिमान में कुछ वित्तीय प्रावधान उपलब्ध कराए जाते हैं। अगर विद्यालय चाहे तो उस वित्तीय प्रावधान के अंतर्गत विद्यार्थियों के लिए आवश्यक सेवाएँ जुटा सकता है। कई विद्यालय ऐसा कर रहे है, लेकिन अधिकांशतः उसका उचित प्रयोग करने में 'बेबस' और 'लाचार' प्रतीत होते हैं। जबकि इस धन राशि को 'रैंप' आदि बनवाने में भी इस्तेमाल किया जा सकता है। सर्व शिक्षा अभियान के अन्तर्गत प्रारंभिक स्कूली शिक्षकों को हर साल पाँच सौ रूपए दिए जान का प्रावधान है ताकि वे विद्यार्थियों के लिए आवश्यक शिक्षण सामग्री जुटा सकें, बना सकें। शिक्षकों के एक बड़े वर्ग को इसमें भी समस्या आती है कि वे इसे कैसे खर्च करें। अनेक शिक्षकों के पास अपनी पाठ्य-पुस्तकें नहीं होतीं, वे बच्चों से

माँगकर पढ़ाते हैं। वे पाँच सौ रूपए में से अपनी पाठ्य-पुस्तकें तो खरीद ही सकते हैं, लेकिन यह सोच भी नदारद है। सरकारी तंत्र में सुविधाएँ तो काफी हैं लेकिन समय की पाबंदी का अभाव-सा प्रतीत होता। पाँच सौ रूपये अकसर मार्च में मिलते हैं, जब शैक्षिणिक सत्र समाप्ति के अंतिम चरण पर होता है। इस स्थिति से बाकी चीजों--पाठ्य-पुस्तकों, वर्दी आदि के बारे में अनुमान सहज रूप से लगाया जा सकता है।

उपर्युक्त संपूर्ण चर्चा के आधार पर यह प्रश्न उठता है कि सरकारी विद्यालयों की ढाँचागत सुविधाएँ 'सामान्य' विद्यार्थियों को तो मुहैया नहीं है--फिर विशेष आवश्यकता वाले विद्यार्थियों की आवश्यकताओं को किस प्रकार पूरा किया जा सकेगा। वास्तव में समोवशी शिक्षा का क्रियान्वयन करने के लिए जरूरी है कि शिक्षा-तंत्र को मजबूत बनाया जाए। सभी विद्यार्थियों की आधारभूत आवश्यकताओं को पूरा किया जाए और उन्हें मूलभूत सुविधाएँ मुहैया कराई जाए। इन सबसे अतिरिक्त यह भी जरूरी है कि व्यक्तियों को संवेदनशील बनाया जाए। 'संवेदनशीलता का अभाव' अशक्त बच्चों के समक्ष सबसे बड़ी चुनौती है। अवसरों की असमानता, संसाधनों की कमी अथवा संसाधनों का सदुपयोग न होना, मूल्यांकन, शिक्षा संबंधी व्यवस्था में पहल व परिवर्तन की कमी, शिक्षा के अन्य अभिकरणों से अलगाव वाला रवैया आदि कुछ ऐसी समस्याएँ है, जो समावेशी शिक्षा के प्रभावी क्रियान्वयन के समक्ष फैली पड़ी हैं। इन समस्याओं का व्यावहारिक समाधान जुटाना सभी की सामूहिक ज़िम्मेदारी है। समुदाय में भी संवेदनशीलता विकसित करनी होगी, जिससे वे अपनी सक्रिय भागीदारिता सुनिश्चित कर सकें। शिक्षकों में वे कुशलताएँ, योग्यताएँ और सकारात्मक दृष्टिकोण विकसित करने की जरूरत है, जिससे वे कक्षा में समस्त बच्चों को उसी रूप में स्वीकार कर सकें, उनकी क्षमताओं का भरपूर उपयोग कर सकें। साथ ही ऐसी वैकल्पिक शिक्षण-पद्धतियों मूल्यांकन-प्रविधियों का विकास कर सकें जिससे कक्षा के सभी बच्चों में समरसता, सामंजस्य का संचार हो सके। उनमें धैर्य, सहिष्णुता, निष्ठा, स्वीकृति और सद्भावना पुष्पित, पल्लवित हो सके। समाज की मुख्यधारा से अलग-अलग बच्चे स्वयं पर भरोसा कर सकें, आत्म-सम्मान और मनोबल बढ़ा सकें। शुरूआत कहाँ से हो--स्वयं से।

7

Management of Support System for Special Needs in Inclusive Education

Dr. Rita Malhotra

In 1988, the UNESCO constitution on special education, recognized inclusive education as a major issue for future action. The objective was "If we succeed in creating effective learning situations for disabled persons within the ordinary school system, we also prepare the ground for an educationally ideal situation for all pupils." UNESCO in the nineties, at the level of planning and policy, led to a "Teacher Education Project—Special Needs in the Classroom" and came out with "The Teacher Education Resource Pack." The "World Conference on Special Needs Education" held in Salamanca (June 1994), addressed the shortfall in special educational provision globally and the ways in which improvements can be made. Inclusior refers to a respect for rights and freedom and implies full citizenship for persons with disabilities. The fundamental arguments for inclusive education are not only educational, but also have solid social and moral concerns.

- Legally it ensures equality of educational opportunities.
- Morally it reduces isolation and prejudice enhancing understanding of deviations.
- From a socio-cultural perspective, it increases the contribution of persons with disabilities to the society at large.
- Educationally it provides positive models of teaching for all children—bringing the advanced technology and teaching strategies of special education to the regular classroom.

The first form of society, that is, *the* school must learn to accept physical differences and deviations in learning styles to accept persons with disabilities in the community. "The secret of education lies in respecting the pupil," says Emerson. We must not dwell on limitations. We must focus on possibilities.

The ultimate aim of education is to prepare a child for a productive, happy and useful adult life. The necessary support provisions to meet the special needs of children in regular schools are:

1. Leadership with a Vision

- For developing an interdisciplinary team approach.
- Authentic Assessment leading to SMART educational goals –
  - Specific
  - Measurable
  - Acceptable
  - Realistic and Within
  - Time Frame.

2. Good Classroom Practices

- Multi-level instruction.
- Cooperative learning.
- Activity based learning.
- Peer tutoring for effective teaching and building self-esteem.
- Use of educational technology.
- Group work.
- Competition between groups and not so much between individuals (syndicate system).

3. Models of Inclusive Practices are:

- Co-teaching Model.
- Parallel Teaching.
- Co-teaching Consultant Model.
- Team Model.
- Resource Teacher Model.

4. Funding

5. Effective Parental Involvement

6. **Positive Attitude and Commitment of the Teacher**

7. **Adapted Curriculum**

If the mutually dependent components of our social system, the child, the parent and the professional can be oriented about complexities of locational, social, physical and curricular integration then this challenging field can be certainly overcome. One teacher cannot have all the expertise required by all children. Consultation and collaboration are key concepts in developing support systems, collaborative assistance and cooperative problem solving.

Suggestions for Programme Modifications

1. Modifications of the environment.
2. Modifications of teaching approaches and modes of instruction.
3. Modifications of instructional materials.
4. Modifications of student's receptive modes.
5. Modifications of student's assignments and evaluation strategies.
6. Modifications of behaviour management approaches and intervention styles.

There are Certain Essentials of School Set-up for Inclusion

The most important are:

- The positive attitude of the Principal to give it a try.
- The Resource room facility with Remedial Teacher and all the resources of teaching technologies along with Teaching Learning Materials (TLM).
- Enhancement of teacher training programmes for curricular modifications, adaptation of content and teaching appliances.

All children are special in one way or another. Children differ and their needs vary considerably. Change is terrifying and some balancing tests must be applied if a policy of inclusion has to be universalized. Children with special needs do require a systematic and intense instruction, quite uncommon in regular classrooms. These tests are:

- The Educational Benefit Test.

- The Impact on the Regular Class Test.
- The Non-academic Benefit Test.
- The Cost-Test.

All these considerations must be evaluated. The Biwako Millenium Framework for action towards an inclusive, barrier free and rights based society for persons with disabilities in Asia and the Pacific" and the UNDP Project on "Education with Zero Rejection" are commendable efforts towards a justified goal. "Inclusive Education" can thrive if it gets the backing of special education principles and strategies to support the regular teachers through a comprehensive model of resource support for all types of disabilities. Amar Jyoti has developed one such model of "Holistic Approach to Education" in which child is at the centre and all his/her developmental needs are fulfilled with understanding and compassion, under an appropriate infrastructure and physical facilities. Such a model if replicated at state levels as Resource Centre, and then it can be of immense value. In the year of the Disabled Persons, 1981 Amar Jyoti Charitable Trust started a school with the pioneering concept of integration and inclusion. The school has both able-bodied and physically challenged children studying together till class VIIIth. After passing the eighth grade, they are assisted to get admission in regular schools for further studies. Those who are not academically inclined are guided into vocational and academic courses affiliated to the National Institute of Open Schooling.

Amar Jyoti School — A Profile

- 600 Children.
- NCERT curriculum supplemented with vocational training.
- Singular goal of all-round personality with self-confidence.
- Free mid-day meal.
- Free medical care.
- Child-centered approach to meet special needs under the same roof.
- Accessibility is the unique feature.

Holistic Approach to Education

Physical Needs

- Medical and Therapeutic Unit.

- Workshop for Assistive Devices.
- Custom made mobility aids.

Psychological and Emotional Needs

- Child Guidance Clinic for assessment and managing strategies.
- Remedial Interventions.
- Home Training Programme (HTP).
- Parent Training.

Socializations

- Play, sing, dance, eat and argue together and develop socializing skills.
- Group celebrations inculcate appropriate social behaviour in community functions and social gatherings.

Medical, Surgical and Therapeutic Support

- Coordinated by School Social Worker.
- Voluntary surgeons perform corrective surgeries.
- Occupational, Physical and Speech therapy.

Guidance and Counselling Services

- Social worker links the family of the child and the teacher.
- Behaviour Modification Strategies.
- Home visits.

Personality Development

- Rich and varied experiences.
- Co-curricular activities develop self-esteem and a coordinated personality.
- Low achievers also get a sense of participation and feeling of success in extracurricular activities.

Recreational and Leisure Time Activities

- Leisure time skills are important living skills.
- National Integrated Sports Meet.
- Special Olympics.

Special Talents

- Abilympics.
- Painting.
- Amar Jyoti Band.
- Group Singing.

Early Intervention

- Home Training and Parental Participation.
- Individual work.
- Group Sessions.
- Parents Orientation and Training (IGNOU-Module).
- Parent Support Group (Aradhana and Swalamban).

Creativity

- Artistic talents are encouraged.
- Poems, stories, jokes find place in "Badte Kadam" a school magazine.

Educational Needs

- Basic for all achievements.
- High achievers are facilitated for higher education.
- Slow learners work on IEPs.
- Partial Integration Programme provides bridges for inclusion.
- Remedial help through CGC Case Conferences.

Guidance for Higher Academics

Scholorships Organised Through Sponsors

- Pankaj achieved over 85 per cent marks in Class VIII. Was awarded Ratanlal Malhotra Scholarship for studying in a Public School.
- Meenakshi for residential programme at Scindia School, Gwalior—She is a trained teacher and is working as a teacher in a Government School.
- Laxmi—for HMT watch repairing and Beauty Parlour—now working as an instructor in Amar Jyoti.
- Shahina Mallik—Studied in Amar Jyoti School and went to

regular College. She came back for doing Diploma in Special Education and is teaching in Amar Jyoti School.

- Ajay Jain – A slow learner passed 10th class through NIOS.

Pre-Vocational

Children are guided:

- to improve self-confidence.
- to develop proper work habits.
- to ensure smooth transition after school to work environment.
- to develop peoples' skills to get along with peers and supervisors.
- to improve opportunity for job placement.

Placement Unit

This unit was setup with the aim to provide job opportunities to persons with disabilities. The registered candidates are made aware of several employment avenues in Corporate and Public sectors, in addition to self-employment opportunities. They are counselled and guided for training as well as employment.

Vocational Courses at Amar Jyoti

- Maintenance and Repair of Common Electrical Appliances.
- Diploma Course in Industrial Electronics.
- Integrated Textile and Fashion Designing.
- Cutting Tailoring and Dress Making.
- Weaving and Spinning.
- Computer.
- Carpentry.
- Beauty Culture.

NIOS Vocational Courses at Amar Jyoti

- Cutting Tailoring and Dress Making.
- Bakery and Confectionery.
- Computer (MS Word).
- Beauty Culture.

Teachers are very important in the life of all children. All Amar Jyoti teachers have undergone training in Special Education. The

Centre for Special Education in the campus runs training programmes and teachers are sponsored one by one to under go the training for the benefit of all children in the school. For the purpose of training teachers and parents of Children with special needs, a series of eight Mainstreaming Books and a Curriculum Guide for Individualized Programme of Intellectually Challenged were published as resource materials.

8

Facilitating Inclusive Education: The Challenges in Teacher Preparation

Dr. Swati Sanyal

The development in Special Education over the years has been slow but steady. Before 1900, Institutions for persons with disabilities were mostly managed by voluntary efforts and missionaries. The charity approach was predominant during those days which gave birth to a model of custodial care, causing extreme segregation of people with disabilities.

Where are we Today

- 200 million School Age Children.
- 4 million children with special education needs.
- Only 3500 schools for persons with different disabilities.
- 1974 Government of India introduces scheme of Integrated Education.
- By year 2000 over 90000 disabled students enrolled in general schools.
- SSA envisages free and compulsory education for all children up to 14 years age by 2010.

Huge Task Ahead of Us

After independence in 1947, the human rights approach started gaining ground and provision for services to persons with disabilities found place in the constitution itself. Initially special school approach was considered to be the most effective strategy and as a result scores of special schools emerged. Currently it is estimated that there are over three thousand five hundred special schools for persons with different disabilities. The exact numbers of special schools are not fully known as there are many NGOs running such schools, which are not included in the directories. As most of these special schools are concentrated in urban areas, children with disabilities in rural areas do not get adequate access to special education services.

A startling figure indicated, in the seminar on special education, at the Asia Pacific Programme of Education and Information Development, Japan (November 6 - 10, 2000) that only 5 per cent of children with disabilities are enrolled in schools. Moreover, 40 per cent of children with disabilities are found to be not completing 5 years of basic education whereas 20 per cent children are found to be not completing the further 3 years of compulsory education.

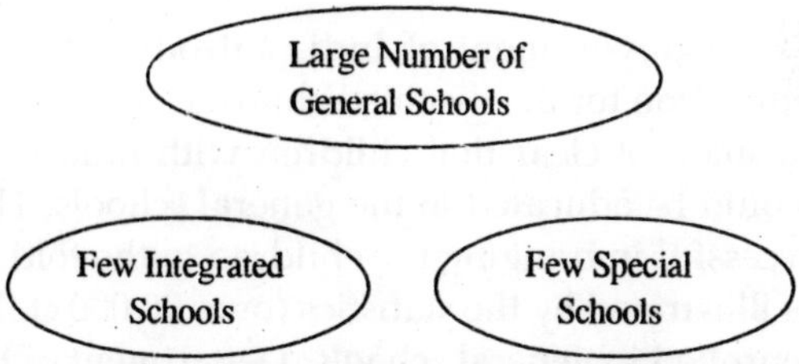

The Office of the Chief Commissioner of Persons with Disabilities stated that not more than 4 per cent of children with disabilities have access to education. Whatever may be the case, the enactment of legislation by Government has helped in facilitating access to education for all learners with SEN by introducing various entitlements like scholarship, allowances, reservations etc. The right of every child to education was strongly advocated by the Jometien World Declaration on Education for All (1990). Also the Standard Rules in the equalization of opportunities for Persons with Disabilities (1993) was an important resolution to improve the educational scenario for persons with disabilities. This had major implications for the Indian situation which initiated three legislative initiatives—The Rehabilitation Council of India Act, 1992; The Persons with Disabilities (Equal Opportunities, Protection of Rights and Full Participation) Act, 1995 and the National Trust for Welfare of Persons with Autism, Cerebral Palsy, Mental Retardation and Multiple Disabilities Act, 1999. These acts are different in their scope but nevertheless aimed at improving the quality of life of the persons with different disabilities through comprehensive education scheme.

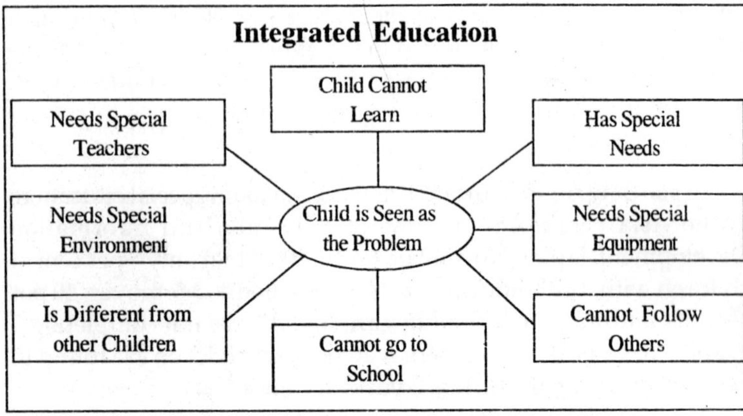

In 1974, the Government of India introduced a scheme of integrated education for the disabled children. This opened many avenues and made it clear that children with mild to moderate disabilities could be educated in the general schools. The scheme has been successful in bringing the children to the fold of general education as illustrated by the statistics (over 90,000 children with disabilities enrolled in general schools: Department of Education, 2000). Even though a number of children with disabilities have been integrated in regular schools, the great majority of children in rural areas do not receive appropriate education. The reason for this could be many but it became imperative to make this a human rights issue and this set the stages for further changes in the philosophy of educational access through provision of inclusive education.

To provide quality education to all learners, NCF, 2000, brought out by the NCERT, recommended inclusive schools for all without specific reference to pupils with SEN. *Segregation or isolation is good neither for learners with disabilities nor for general learners without disabilities. Social requirement is that learners with special needs should be educated along with other learners in inclusive schools which are cost effective and have sound pedagogical practices* (NCERT, 2000).

In its broadest and all encompassing meaning, inclusive education, as an approach, seeks to address the learning needs of all children, youth and adults with a specific focus on those who are vulnerable to marginalization and exclusion. It implies all learners, young people—with or without disabilities being able to learn

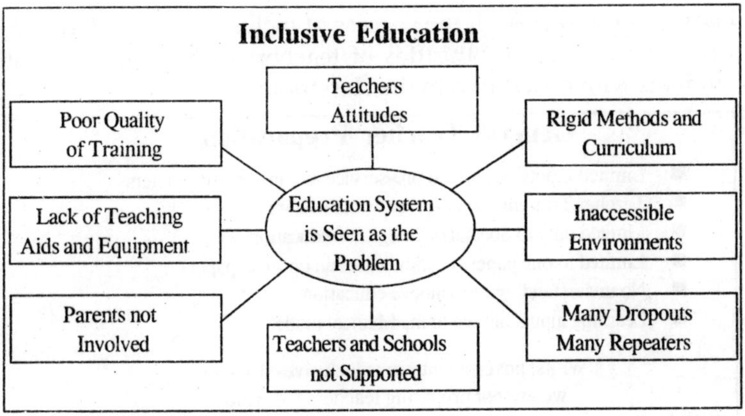

together through access to common pre-school provisions, schools and community educational setting with an appropriate network of support services. This is possible only in a flexible education system that assimilates the needs of a diverse range of learners and adapts itself to meet these needs. It aims at all stakeholders in the system (learners, parents, community, teachers, administrators and policy makers) to be comfortable with diversity and see it as a challenge rather than a problem. (Comprehensive Action Plan for Inclusion in Education of Children and Youth with Disabilities, 2005 issued by MHRD.)

Truly enough, the inclusion of children with diversity as well as the movement to keep students with disabilities in general education environment present education with a new challenge. The challenge is now, to bring changes in teachers' values, attitudes, professional expertise and knowledge. It also signifies that a sea change is required in the professionals who are responsible for training of teachers.

Present Scenario

In our country the concept of inclusive education has not yet been linked to a broader discussion of pedagogy (Anita, 2000). As inclusive education becomes more widespread, significantly more students will require specialized support in the general education classrooms. Consequently, there is an increasing need for both general and special education teachers who will be able to teach students with or without disabilities in inclusive classrooms. Teachers set the tone of the classrooms and as such the success of inclusion may well depend upon the prevailing attitudes of teachers as they interact with students with disabilities in the classrooms.

General Teacher Preparation

- Limited inputs on SEN to pre-service and in-service teachers
- Teacher Training varying from state to state
- Limited only to Special or Integrated education
- Limited to one paper (in some cases an optional paper)
- No understanding of inclusive education
- Learning inputs limited to the Medical model

Whilst government wants inclusive education
we are not preparing teachers for same.

This has implication for preparation of all education personnel. Since the teachers will be primarily responsible for bringing about this radical change, urgent reflection and revision of both general and special education courses are needed for capacity building and making inclusive education a reality.

A study was conducted by Singhal and Rouse (2003) to find out the practitioner's perspective on inclusive education. Many of these teachers stated that there have been no changes in their teaching and also justified that by pointing to various constraints like large class sizes, task of maintaining discipline, vast amount of syllabus. Some of them also mentioned that the included student was just one of many in the class.

The open file on Inclusive Education (UNESCO, 2001) suggests that the following demands be placed on teachers from the perspective of inclusive curricula:

- They have to become involved in curriculum development at the local level and they have to be skilled in curriculum adaptation in their own classrooms.
- They have to manage a complex range of classroom activities.
- They have to know how to support their students learning without giving them predetermined answers.
- They have to work outside traditional subject boundaries and in culturally sensitive ways.

In almost all Indian Universities, general and special education programmes exist under a dual system. That is, the various teachers training programmes still use a model that ensures separation between general and special education teacher preparation. Teachers' training is thus segregated with each discipline being viewed as different and special.

Special Teacher Preparation

- Teachers for special classrooms teaching children with SEN
- Resource or itinerant teachers (separate from General Education classrooms)
- Inadequate Teacher preparation for Inclusive Education
- Inclusion Demands A New Emphasis on Teacher Preparation

A further limitation of this separate teachers' training model is that the University Teacher Preparation Programmes overemphasize knowledge acquisition than equipping teachers with practical skills for teaching a diverse range of students including those with disabilities. As a result researchers have identified inadequate or inappropriate field based experiences and lack of exposure to children with disabilities in many pre-service programmes.

It would be appropriate to mention here the findings of a study conducted by NCERT (Julka, 2004) for strengthening of teacher education curriculum of DIETs from the perspective of learners with special educational needs.

The major findings of the study are:

- Teacher Training inputs at pre-service level and those at in-service level do include inputs on learners with SEN but these vary from State to State and are very limited in scope.
- The inputs as such are not adequate to develop competencies in teachers for teaching in an inclusive classroom.
- The inputs both in theory and practice are limited and reflect upon special and integrated education.
- In pre-service programmes, the inputs or learners with SEN are either covered under one Unit of a compulsory paper or are covered in an optional paper. The optional paper is not very popular with the trainees because of unavailability of trained educators and resource material.
- The teacher educators do not yet possess the skills to support

effective inclusive learning. Neither the teacher educators understand the meaning of inclusive education, nor are there any related curricular inputs.

- Most of the inputs were limited to learners with disabilities and fitted with the perspective denoted by the medical model.
- The curriculum inputs in no state were designed from the perspective of inclusive education or based on social model.

Thus the result show that on one hand all governmental efforts are directed towards bringing all children to school through the major programmes like the DPEP and SSA, on the other hand, even the peripheral coverage of practical issues in teacher education are absent. At the same time success of inclusive education does not only depend on general classroom teachers as is commonly perceived. The preparation of special teachers to facilitate inclusion is equally important.

In 1995, the persons with Disabilities (Equal Opportunities, Protection of Rights and Full Participation) Act, reiterated the need for trained manpower to teach in integrated schools and called on Governments to set-up adequate number of Teachers' Training Institutions and assist the National Institute and Voluntary Organizations to develop teachers training programmes specializing in disabilities so that sufficient support is available for these children. The Rehabilitation Council of India is taking major initiatives in standardizing and recognising a number of certificate, diploma and degree programmes in the field of special teacher preparation.

Gaps in the Present System

- Lack of Conceptual Clarity among both General and Special Teachers
- Lack of practical exposure to teaching in Inclusive Classroom
- Neither set of teachers are equipped to handle the other set of students
- Neither set of teachers willing to accept the responsibility for all students
- Too few teachers to take responsibility of children with SEN.

Due to a history of separation, inclusion causes uncertainty about the roles and responsibilities of general classroom teachers and special education teachers. Inclusion demands definition of roles and responsibilities to avoid conflict and confusion among general and special teachers. In an inclusive model special educators need to operate as a team in many aspect of their role. As teaming skills are recognized as learned behaviours that typically require direct instruction, training in collaborative skill should be an integral part of teacher preparation curriculum. Working as a part of a team requires new roles and understandings. Teamwork require general and special teachers to share, cooperate and agree on methods of instruction, materials, discipline, evaluation and other matters. There are many advantages to teamwork that are not apparent until they have been experienced. Unfortunately now-a-days there is a general tendency to deride special education set-ups as being segregated, isolated, expensive, restricting. I would however like to emphasize that the relevancy of any system is entirely dependent on larger educational, social and economic context. Any discussion about our country needs to be placed within the over all perspectives of massive numbers, social, cultural and economic diversity, limited resources, competing priorities and supply. I would like to harp on the fact with this kind of scenario a close collaboration between general and special teacher preparation programme should be encouraged. The collaboration between the National Council of Teacher Education and the Rehabilitation Council of India will make this role and responsibility of general and special teacher more inclusive.

The National Focus Group on Education of Children with Special Needs for National Curriculum Framework 2005, has given the following recommendations for teacher education:

- Gear all teacher education programmes (both pre-service and in-service) to developing the pedagogical skills required in inclusive classrooms.
- Correlate the style of teaching to the learning styles of all children.
- Make the class teacher responsible for all the children in the class. In case special support is required on account of SEN, this should be in the form of assistance to the class teacher.
- Regard all special teachers in a given school as full-fledged members of the school community.
- For effective delivery of education in the inclusion mode, all teacher education (in-service and pre-service) must be restructured.

- To inculcate respect for diversity and the concept of an inclusive society the teacher education programmes and the curriculum framework should incorporate a component of human rights education.

Conclusion

From the above discussion we can find out certain gaps in the present system of teacher preparation.

- Lack of conceptual clarity about inclusive education among both general and special teachers.
- Lack of practical exposure to teaching in inclusive classroom.
- Neither general nor special teachers are equipped to handle diversity in the classrooms.
- Neither set of teachers is willing to accept the responsibility for ALL students.

Some Suggestions to Meet the Challenge

- To make the concept of Inclusive Education clear to:
  — Teacher Educators
  — General Teachers
  — Special Teachers
- Curricular inputs to be designed from the perspective of Social Model.
- Practical Exposure both at pre and in-service levels:
  — To General teachers to handle diversity in classrooms.
  — To Special teachers to handle large classrooms
- Emphasize concept of Team Work between General and Special Teachers.

From Yours and Mine to OURS

Some suggestions to meet the challenge of teacher preparation are:

- General teachers must learn methods and curricular modifications that respond to the diverse learning needs of all students in classroom.
- Practical exposure both at pre-and in-service levels,
  1. to general teachers to handle diversity in classroom,
  2. to special teachers to handle large classrooms.
- Incorporate a component of human rights education in teacher education programmes.
- To consider the extension of duration of teacher training programmes at B.Ed. level.

- When providing sensitizing courses to general teachers, special attention should be paid to development of teaching-learning material required for different categories of students as well as classroom management.
- Emphasize concept of Team Work between general and special teachers.
- Continuous rehabilitation education for teacher educators and school administrators.

In brief we can conclude that to make inclusive education successful all teacher preparation curriculum needs to be more broad based to equip the trainee teachers to take account of the individual needs of all learners. They should be able to come out of the mindset of looking at children as mine or yours.

The journey of Inclusion is from yours and mine to ours.

9

A Parent's Journey from Exclusion to Inclusion: Implications for Regular Schools

Dr. Shyama Chona

I have been introduced as the principal of DPS, R.K. Puram and a founder member of Tamanna but one thing that was forgotten is that I am the mother of Tamanna. I am not here in the capacity of a special educator, my doctorate is in English not in special education. So, dear friends, you are much more educated than I am because my field is plain and simple education. But, I think my gift of God cannot be greater than all the awards and prizes and that gift is my own daughter Tamanna. What I have learnt from her is much greater than my Ph.D, being principal of DPS, R.K. Puram, because I think that special children are truly gifted and when you as teachers get opportunity to be in their company, you also get a part of that gift. I have reared her and brought her up as if I have little Goddess in my home. Time and again, I have said in conferences and meets, we are constantly talking about IQ that is intelligent quotient; we are talking about PQ that is physical quotient, EQ that is emotional quotient but there are two more quotients S^2Q. For me these are spiritual and social quotient. We want integration for these children because they are already very high in spiritual quotient but you cannot leave them alone and they need to live in real world. Thirty years ago, when my daughter was born, I took her to a number of schools. The moment the principal saw me, she said, "Oh my God, this school is for high achievers, what are you doing with your daughter here." Then, I tried to tell her that her smile, her bewitching eyes, her desire to learn is as much as the desire of any other child. Could you please admit her? She said, " I am sorry, the reputation of my school will be destroyed. What will the parents say that I have taken a girl who looks so weird but to me I think she is really a little Goddess. I went pillar to post, I would not really name the schools, but nobody was ready to accept her. I had to take her to US where at the age of nine, she learnt to stand. She was somehow registering but she couldn't swallow, so she was throwing out all the saliva. She had a head thrust, her tongue was out, her eye was squint, and head was tilted as well. People thought that she was funny looking, but I thought she was as good as anybody else. I am speaking from the heart of a mother.

So, when American society loved her for her smile and said, "Mrs. Chona, you are a professional. Why don't you get her adopted here?" We are ready to take her and keep her here, I said, "No way, but you please help me to make her stand, walk, talk, learn." They did a prognosis for her. I suffered the Indian way of life and now I was going to get another set back, and the set back was, "yes, she will walk, she will talk, she will swallow, but sorry she's only trainable, she will not get educated. Ladies and Gentlemen, I want to tell that Tamanna is today a teacher at Delhi Public School. She has just performed a solo at FICCI with eight poor children for she wanted to do something great in her life. She is a product of integrated education starting at the age of ten. Until the age of ten, I had nothing but after ten, I realized that she had been absorbing but she had no means to express herself. She could not walk or talk but once I joined DPS for her sake and I took her in, I changed my own career from a college lecturer and permanent employee of UGC to teaching in a school i.e. DPS; I realized that Tamanna was gaining confidence, because we were not making her feel low about herself. I am coming to values that we give to child before learning takes place. So one day she said, "mummy the children here did a particular gesture when they see me." I said, "Tamanna, when do they do this to you and in two years 'Hello' in DPS, R.K. Puram was turned into Tamanna Hello. All normal boys and girls were saying 'Hello' to each other and it was 'Tamanna Hello."

We think that these children can't be educated, they can't be made independent economically, feasible to do work and we start predetermining their future also. It is to understand that they have same joys, same sorrows, same dreams and may be there is brain damage, those cells cannot be made alive. But, surely with special education and with social interaction they can do much more than they have done or they are thought of having done. So, when I put her in DPS, she would sit in the class, but she was not able to do certain subjects like math. Before that, she spent few months in another school, the Junior End High School. I bought her a calculator. We started taking her to bank and shops. Whatever, she was taking in without getting into much of writing work absorption was taking place. She amazed her teachers with her memory because she did not know the ways of world and her whole concentration was on her learning. She knew somewhere in sub-conscious that she had missed ten years of her life. Everything teacher said was meaningful. She was learning geography, as she couldn't understand it, she used to say why the world was round. I couldn't make her understand. I gave up some things in physics and chemistry. What she could really learn was her excellent language expression and started writing few poems here and there. It has been my greatest miracle of life. I get a gulp in my throat when I talk to all of you. But, I think education be it B.Ed or anything else, is necessary. Its not about special schools, not about normal schools, it is about people, education is about the people. Like in the world, we all look different. I don't think there is any creation where two faces are alike, similarly no two brains are the same. We have to strengthen the strengths and weaken the weaknesses in education system. Every education must look at the individual profile of children in the classroom. After the profile has been fully understood, nourish the child academically, emotionally, psychologically, socially and spiritually according to the needs of the child.

Yes, there are problems in our country. Our class size is very large even in public schools like mine; we have 30-35 children in the junior school and 38-40 in the senior school. So when there are 1 or 2 kids in a class, certainly teachers require more time to deal with these children. They need to understand what they are all about and what should be the right IEP that is Individual Educational Programme. You require conferences and conference should be attended by regular teachers, special teachers, physiotherapist, speech therapist, special educator and principal of the school, because the key person in promoting integrated education in any country esp. India is the principal of the school. If, principal of the school has never ever imagined or experienced what disability is then that empathy, that sympathy, that oneness with the cause is missing. I propose that principals in schools should be first liberated from their ideas, become broad minded only then can they lead the way for the teachers.

The special teacher or educator should be more than the regular teacher because he/she has a greater challenge. Yes, the child will not learn everything that is taught in the class and the child has to be a part of the resource centre. So the schools require good resource centres, where that subjects which is not possible for the child to go through in the class, is taken away and one to one education is imparted, therapy is given of all kinds, then I am sure there will be many many successful Tamannas in the world. It is a very sad thing that the special children or children with special needs are not included in the ministry of education. They are still under the ministry of social justice and empowerment. This proves that disability sector is still not receiving the social justice that it should receive and also proves that we have to empower the 10 per cent of the total population of this country, for the statistics have said that there are those many in our world that need special help. I have something beautiful, which I will read to you;

To be a part, and not stand apart
To belong and not to be isolated
To be accepted and not accommodated
To have opportunities and not favours
Is to be really included.

"We want to be a part of the education system of this country. We can work towards our own social justice. We have the ability, capacity, and potential." I am sure you all agree that these we are the disabled of this nation who are actually waiting to be recognized because the amount of strength they have we may not have.

In DPS today I have seventeen blind children and they set the pace of the whole class. If they walk fast, I put them right in the beginning of the class. When they go out, they have a buddy, a friend who leads them around. This buddy is, I think more enlightened than anybody else does. Seventeen of them have seventeen buddies, they take them to the bus, to lab, they take them everywhere. Then I have children who are on the wheel chair. We did not have ramps earlier, and we are getting them now. We have given a .... To the son of my driver who is a spastic. You know students of class XI go to help him up in the evening to run the...in the hostel. The sky is the limit, but first we have to change our mindset. We think to look at somebody who is different is a sin. We think if we hold the hand of somebody who requires our help, we are doing charity. I don't think so! If the 90 per cent of people want to be healthy, happy and feel terrific they have to make the rest 10 per cent also to be partners in their joy, happiness and their celebration. No society will be called an awakened society; no society will be called enlightened society until and unless everybody in that society has made to that right to joy, right to live and right to live well in an integrated manner. That is the key to our life existence. I have very often discussed the matter to higher authorities and policy makers and have repeatedly said, 'Let's not be rigid in our policies and if we have policies, let us not make policies for the sake of the world to see." Yes, in India also now we have reservation for 3-5 per cent of the disabled. I still think that educational administrators have to understand the low priority that is being given to the disabled of this nation. The resistance in the school system should be defied. Who can do it— You will do it!

'I am, I can, and I will' should be the motto of every teacher. I think we require appropriate support services for these children, meanwhile they are journeying or travelling or climbing wherever. If we are a great nation, it can become greater not just by increasing our national productivity and income but by being more human and humane. There is no doubt that there is dearth of infrastructure required for inclusion. We can only have inclusion when we have better mindset, better infrastructure and facilities required. There is also lack of awareness for centuries. These children have been hidden in the cupboards, and under the beds. You go to a home where there is a disabled child, before the mother opens the door; she tells others to hide her. If a girl has to get married and she has a younger sister who is disabled the mother thinks her daughter will not get married, so take the other one far away so that she is not seen. When the child has to be born in a family because of lack of awareness the pregnant mother thinks, "my husband has a disabled brother or sister, I may not bring another disabled child into the world. These are myths and these myths can only be replaced if we do great awareness campaigns and bring the facts out. I think all that we do in this world, all the prayers that we actually offer to God would not be as magnanimous as they can be if we served those who need us and that's why they are those who are called 'people with special needs.'

I think the society can become a greater place to live in. The world will be some place where you would want to belong if you had done some good task in your life. I know special children will always need human endeavour, however hard you may try they still will be needing family and the community support for which, are we ready? There is a big difference between India and the West. In India, we do have a very good family support. In the west when a baby is born with special needs, it becomes the responsibility of the state or the nation. In our country, it is the family that suffers and suffers and suffers!

You as teachers can help these families to come out of these problems if you are ready to lead a greater help. I hope the inclusion of this paper in the B.Ed. is actually a task which should be taken seriously and whenever you get an opportunity to teach these children, please take the first step because this is a very very long journey and I am happy that I am in the middle of the journey!

Thank you.

10

Inclusion of Individuals with Specific Learning Difficulties: Contextualization to Pedagogical Issues and Vocationalization

Dr. Renu Malaviya

The need to focus on, 'Education for all', started emerging in Britain and America, at the end of 1950's and early 1960's. Thus, the difficulties that many children were facing with the conventional teaching-learning processes began to attract serious attention. An increasing number of children were found unable to cope with the school work specifically with reading, writing and mathematics. These children were otherwise bright, fairly articulate in their verbal expressions and did not appear to have any form of intellectual impairment, sensory handicap or visual impairment. On April 6th, 1963, Dr. Samuel Kirk addressed a gathering of anxious parents in Chicago, at which he first used the term learning disabilities to describe these children:

> *This meeting is not concerned with the children who have sensory handicaps, such as the deaf or the blind, with the children who are mentally retarded. It is concerned with the children who see and hear and who do not have marked intellectual deficits, but who show deviations in behaviour and in psychological development to such an extent that they are unable to adjust in the home or to learn by ordinary methods in schools.*

The term Learning Difficulties (LD) if one looks at the literature is often used also to include slow learners and other intellectual impairment. Teachers in the Indian schools often use the term, 'slow learners' for the child with dyslexia, dyscalculia, dysgraphia etc. They often tend to interpret the term as children who take time to learn. Of course, they may often not be focusing upon the limitations of their own instructional strategies which cause these children difficulties in output of information as the school system wants. This also often leads to the assumption that these individuals are intellectually challenged. Hence most contemporary definitions have emphasized upon the fact that these are individuals with average to superior intelligence.

Beginning with Orton's coining of the term SLD (Specific Learning Difficulties) in the year 1925 and also linking it with the above arguments and many other related data it becomes highly pertinent that the shift towards the terminology SLD (i.e., Specific Learning Difficulties) is emphasized rather than LD. Another issue of debate and reflection, currently the theme of many brainstorming sessions in many academic forums, is whether these are Specific Learning Disabilities or Specific Learning Difficulties. A deeper issue centres on a better sensitivity and insight to the art and science of pedagogical issues.

Just to glimpse back a little into the historical perspective of the terms dyslexia, LD, SLD. When the movement towards education for all began in Great Britain, it was found that there were these children who despite normal or above normal intelligence and good conventional methods of classroom teaching-learning processes were not able to learn how to read effectively. They were termed dyslexic from the Greek derivative *Dys* meaning difficulty and *lexia* meaning words. Thus dyslexia literary means *difficulty with words*. Gradually, it was realized that there were another set of children and adults who have difficulty with arithmetic. They came to be termed as individuals with dyscalculia and then came the term dysgraphia meaning difficulty with writing. While in America the term Learning Disability / difficulty emerged almost simultaneously with the term dyslexia, it became an umbrella term for the associated difficulties/ disabilities.

In Britain, the term dyslexia continued to be also used, as an umbrella term for the different difficulties mentioned. Finally, the focus moves on to SLD. The major bodies working in India in this area in the cities of Chennai, Mumbai, Chandigarh and Delhi prefer to focus on the umbrella term SLD. The debate within the circles interested in the welfare of these groups of individuals with reference to whether to use the term disability or difficulty still continues.

As one looks at some contemporary definitions related to dyslexia/SLD, it becomes obvious that the issue has lesser to do with the learning capacity of the individual but rather with the pedagogical transactions within the educational systems. A teacher intern while understanding the pedagogical issues when in training also will use the repertoire of knowledge one had assimilated in one's conscious and sub-conscious being while being a part of the educational processes oneself at school (which is roughly 12 to 14 years and that to at ones' formative years).

Secondly, it will come naturally to anyone be it the teacher educator at the university or the teacher intern or the school teacher to follow those learning and instructional strategies consciously and sub-consciously which had benefited ones learning processes. Hence, it is a task which requires intense reflection and a complete change of mind set and a deep understanding of ones own needs as a teacher to be able to accept, internalize and then support alternative methods of learning and instructional processes.

Any set of hidden 'disabilities' will be difficult for other individuals to accept and understand. As anything that is concrete is easier for the brain to perceive, accept and react to than an abstract construct. The processes involved in the black box of the individual with SLD become difficult for a teacher without SLD to even perceive. In other words, the processes that happens between the input and the output of knowledge constructions (in the black box) are not visible or insightful to a person who does not have SLD.[1] SLD is often thus referred to as a set of hidden disabilities.

The term LD/ SLD is defined as a disorder or difficulty in one or more of the basic processes involved in understanding spoken or written language or it may manifest itself as a variation in one or more of the processes such as thinking, listening, speaking, reading, writing, spelling or mathematics. In other words, these individuals process knowledge differently from the larger population.

The National Joint Council for Learning Disability in 1981 defined it as:

"A generic term that refers to a heterogeneous group of disorders manifested by significant difficulties in the acquisition and use of

listening, speaking, reading, writing, reasoning or mathematical ability. These disorders are intrinsic to the individual and presumed to be due to central nervous system dysfunction, even though a learning disability may occur concomitantly with other handicapping conditions (e.g. sensory impairment, mental, social and emotional disturbances or environmental influences e.g. cultural differences, insufficient/inappropriate instruction and psychogenic factors). It is not the direct result of these conditions or influences."

The Association for Children and Adults with learning Disabilities defines it as:

" Specific Learning Disability (SLD) is a chronic condition of presumed neurological origin which is a selectively interferes with the development integration and /or demonstration of verbal and / or non-verbal abilities. Specific Learning Disabilities (SLD) exists as distinct handicapping conditions in the presence of average to superior intelligence, adequate sensory motor system and adequate learning opportunities. The condition varies in its manifestation and degree of severity."

Hence, SLD is a condition, which exists inspite of average to above intelligence and appropriate conventional teaching pedagogies. Contrast this with a definition of Mental Impairment as stated by the American Association of Mental Deficiency:

"Significant sub average general intellectual functioning resulting in or associated with impairments in adaptive behaviour and manifested during the developmental period."

In India the groups working for and with individuals with SLD do not have their main demands for reservations in jobs, but more towards effective sensitization, appropriate pedagogical issues with examination options and reforms and forums for parent professional corporation. The options requested during the evaluation processes are also from that perspective. In the absence of larger sensitivity in the education community and changes thereby, demand for privileges such as extra hour during examinations, limited number of language to be studied, exemption of arithmetic for individuals with dysgraphia, aware and sensitive examiners are some of the options requested. Examination bodies such as

Central Board of Secondary Education (CBSE) are now sensitive to these issues and have made atleast some provision in that direction.

The CBSE privileges for children with SLD are:

- Exemption from third language (right from the beginning, if required).
- An extra hour during the final examinations.
- 15-20 minutes extra for unit tests.
- Use of scribe (writer). A scribe can be any child in a class. atleast one year below that of the SLD child.

Research in the west as well as in India indicates that nearly 10-15 per cent of the population has specific learning disabilities/ difficulties. Hence in a school of about 4000 children nearly 400-500 children will show signs of SLD. Fortunately the mild forms of SLD are more common than the severe forms. Hence with the relevant inputs in the teacher education programmes and the school and college systems, these individuals can be easily included into the regular classrooms. At this point it also needs to be stated that behavioural problems and loss of self-esteem in these individuals are secondary manifestations and not the primary manifestations and need to be treated as such. It also needs to be focused that such individuals have certain strengths which because of the limitations of our education system often go unnoticed and undeveloped.

As educationist and others are aware:

Inclusion Education means individuals with disability and individuals with non-disability learning together in ordinary pre-schools, provisions, schools, colleges and universities with appropriate networks of supports. Inclusion means enabling pupils to participate in the life and work of mainstream institutions to the best of their abilities, whatever their needs.

Inclusion is a philosophy built on the belief that all people are equal and should be respected and valued as an issue of basic human rights. Inclusion can be viewed as an unending set of processes in which children and adult who are differently abled have the opportunities to participate fully in all activities offered to people who do not have the so-called disabilities.

Inclusion is enabling pupils to participate in the life and work of 'mainstream'[2] institutions to the best of their abilities, what ever their special needs. Hence inclusive classrooms reach out beyond the classroom into the larger community and evoke a sense of belonging to the diverse heterogeneous human family as well as provide a diverse heterogeneous environment to grow and learn. Inclusive education appreciates the unique and diverse characteristics and abilities and capabilities of all its members.

The contemporary paradigm shift has been initiated with the thinking that there are no problem children but problem situations. Hence, the major focus of any difficulty exhibited by the child in learning was not to be attributed to the problem within the child but the limitation of the education system to facilitate learning in the child.

Society is a mosaic of individuals. Each child is different and unique with their strengths and limitations and each of them has a role to play in society as an adult. Hence it is but obvious that it would be a wiser step to have children integrated into the regular schools, colleges and other educational institutes as far as possible as it would prepare them and their counterparts best for an integrated society and life.

Emerging from the above an important paradigm shift is highlighted in the following paragraph.

> *"That any difficulty that in a child exhibited in learning was to be attributed not to a problem within the child, but to the school system. The organizations and management of schools and the various programmes of teaching and interventions could also be one of the causes of the individual's learning difficulties."*

Inclusion however is not advisable without certain infrastructure changes. These could be categorized under:

- Physical.
- Instructional Transactional Processes.
- Psycho-social mindsets.

Inclusive education would be facilitated by certain models of support, special education related services within the society and the education system and of course, the 'in-class support'. The in-class support would consist of embedded support within the educational pedagogies as well as special external support in different settings. These embedded and external support is best when it comes from a team consisting of school personnels, peers, therapists, special education teachers, administrators, psychologist, counsellors, volunteers and other resources.

Research states that Specific Learning Disability (SLD) is a highly heterogeneous group. My direct work with individuals with specific learning difficulties over the past two decades has also shown the heterogeneity within this group. As each one of them is so different from the other the school teachers as per their present training in most Indian Schools, find it very difficult to translate what they learn about one child with SLD that they may be working with in a particular year to another child with SLD in their class the next year. As teacher educators and school teachers and administrators, we need to understand that some of these individuals may have their strength areas in the sciences, others in humanities and still others in the commerce stream. What may be considered, as 'easy subject', for one may actually be a difficult subject for another.

There are these general classroom accommodations for children with SLD. These can be categorized into the following categories:

- Evaluation processes.
- Classroom teaching leaning processes.
- School, family and community networking.

Beyond this there are certain major shifts in paradigms which need to be focussed upon:

1. The Processes of Constructing Knowledge Rather than Knowledge as a Finished Product

In the field of education undoubtedly the focus is shifting from dissemination of knowledge by the expert to the so-called novice to the facilitation of the construction of knowledge. The contemporary need is to understand oneself and to further sensitize the learner to the processes involved in the construction of knowledge and not knowledge as a finished product. This may obviously not be a very easy task, but surely it would lead to better outputs from school education.

In order to gain better insight into the issue of SLD, let us just peep into the major neuro-developmental constructs involved in the construct of knowledge that is involved in school education.

They are:

- Regulation,
- Organization,
- Presentations,
- Interpretation and Implementations, and
- Sophistication.

Regulation is based upon attention, which involves mental energy controls, processing controls and production controls.

Similarly *Organization* consists of *temporal sequential ordering* and spatial ordering. Temporal sequential ordering would further have divisions such as assimilating basic time and seriation concepts and vocabulary, musical rhythms, phonetic segmentation and resynthesis, narrative organization in writing, prioritization and schedule planning, step-wise work and problem solving, appreciation of historical perspective, awareness, perception, memory, output, time management and higher sequential thinking. While *Spatial Ordering* would consist of Spatial awareness, spatial perception, spatial memory, spatial output, material management, higher spatial thinking (visual discriminatory abilities, visual-motor integration, appreciation of visual boundaries, spatial planning in writing, focus on visual details, perceive part/ whole relationships in maths etc., non-verbal reasoning with spatial concepts, graphic representations of knowledge.

Moving on to *Preservation* (Short-term memory, Active working memory, Long-term memory), it would have areas such as deliberate paired associated learning, symbolic visual memory, frequent use of episodic memory, stress on convergent single item recall, procedural sequential recall, storage and recall of multiple directions, rapid simultaneous recall, automatized recall of facts and procedures, use of mnemonic strategies, rapid rule recall, convergent activation of prior knowledge, metamemory sophistication, cumulative recall and so on.

Similarly the other larger areas of neuro-developmental constructs, namely Interpretation and Implementations as well as Sophistication also have so many further smaller constructs.

Now if the school teacher is sensitive to these smaller categories of constructions and after due to teacher-based and finally psychologist based diagnosis transacts in accordance with the information into the learning processes for the individual child, the child does not get labelled and the education system is able to reach to the very root of where learning requires alternate pedagogies.

Lets take a very simple example of an individual who has problem with space management.[3] Such a person may have a problem in the perception of words such as pre- service, or the conceptual differences between a full stop (.) and a comma (,) or an inverted comma ('). Probably in the Hindi language those children who just do not grow out of perceiving the difference between two *matras* of the same group may also be having a space management problem. As school teachers and also scholars of education and psychology, we at times wrongly tend to believe that languages which have a stronger phonetic base are easier for the child with dyslexia or dysgraphia. Research findings with reference to the Hindi language has shown that these individuals face problems in such languages not because of phonetic segmentations related areas but because the individual may have a perceptual variation with space management, or sequential ordering, spatial output or perceived part/whole relationships.

Do I as a school teacher understand those processes or for that matter even the existence of these constructs. Was I anywhere in the B.Ed. programme/other training programme exposed to these constructs and its applications as to how I may transact the school curriculum with their support? For example if I am aware that the child needs special attention in the temporal sequential ordering in the English language or in mathematics, then I as a teacher may find ways and means to facilitate how to evolve or use another path to facilitate it. When the move shifts to identification and dealing with the sub-concepts which hinder further learning processes or which require alternate teaching-learning processes, the very need and reliance on holistic labeling becomes obsolete.

This would also have a direct implication to career counselling and vocationalisation. For example, if the class teacher along with the support from the school counsellor and psychologist finds that expressive language is the limitation and not the strength of the child and fine motor functions and graphomotor functions are the strengths, then the individual's strengths can be directed towards computer graphic related vocationalisation. Or individuals who have strengths in spatial awareness but may have limitations in temporal sequential ordering may be geared towards vocations that predominately focus upon 3-dimenstional perspectives. Probably such an individual would be good in geometry but find the concepts of algebra difficult.

If we the teachers were to change are mindsets about special needs such as dyslexia, dysgraphia, dyscalculia and so on and zero down to more specific specifications, we would be able to address those more effectively in the regular classrooms and hence the number of children with specific learning difficulties who would become highly effective members of the society and with good mental health would increase. No doubt this would mean a better insight and sensitively to enmeshing the different neurodevelopment constructs into the transaction of the school curriculum and link it with a better understanding of the possible career options for the individual.

This would lead to a much better understanding of not only being able to provide individualized instructions in a large group classroom settings for the identified individual with special needs but for all children who would be considered not needing specialized attention.

2. Concept of Small Groups within the Larger Classroom Group: Lesson Planning for Each Individual

In theory the teacher interns may be informed that the teaching-learning processes in the classroom must focus upon each and every child as an individual. Our lesson planning actually plans for a highly homogene group. The physical infrastructure and classroom movements are also not given its due importance. Attempts have been made by me with in-service motivated teachers to evolve lesson plans keeping the heterogeneity within the classroom as an emphasis and simultaneously emphasizing upon multisensory approach. The actual presentation slot of the lesson plan was categorized into 4-5 groups and the class was mentally grouped into these 4-5 groups by the teacher concerned and transactions were planned for these groups which would take place almost simultaneously in the classroom. Attempts were made to plan out vertical, collateral and alternate activities and assignments. Peer tutoring, assistant teachers and resource corners were stressed upon. This did involve a lot of planning with children with different disabilities ranging from visual impairment, auditory impairment, SLD, ADHD and Cerebral Palsy.

What we did not manage to reach out to was an even more challenging group of learners, namely the gifted individual with specific learning difficulties. Such a child as we are all aware is also referred to as a 2 child (twice exceptional). This child is cognitively gifted but can't take in enough information due to auditory, visual, or sensory processing issues.

Teachers were encouraged to preserve these kits for the coming years. Questions that arouse were the school administrators' almost complete insensitivity towards providing space for work area and storage to their teachers. Doctors, Architects, Engineers, Artist all have their own specific set of kit, which is a must identification of a particular profession. Where are the kits of the teachers? Do the teacher education institutes emphasize on its importance or do we ourselves undermine it?

3. Heterogeneous Teaching in All Classrooms: Importance of Resource Kits and Resource Centres in the Lives of Teachers

An engineer has a kit, which they need at work, a architect brings ones own kit for work, a doctor carries ones medial bag. Similarly beginning from the pre-service programme, teachers need to be encouraged to carry a kit consisting of cost effective indigenous multisensory material. The colleges where I have spent more than half my life on this earth, use peer pressures effectively for encouraging teachers to be better at their jobs. Can the same be used to encourage the school and college teachers to have resource kits for different contents?

My class of teacher interns also has a couple of students who are SLD but have not been diagnosed. Have I tried to transact information and knowledge construction in different alternate ways? Trying to state to the teacher interns that you all are at the abstract cognitive levels while your students in school will be at the concrete cognitive levels does not necessarily facilitates them to use multisensory approaches. I simply must reflect upon various alternate methods of transacting within my classroom.

Equipment such as electronic dictionary and thesaurus, alphabet strips, table squares, folders with lots of writing frames and mind maps and of course a quite corner in the classroom are just some of the easier ways of permitting variations within the classroom.

Every child is unique. When students are diverse, teachers can either "teach to the middle", or face the challenge of diversifying their instruction. Nearly all teachers believe that it's better to differentiate instruction, – but the challenge lies in translating that belief into action. This is what an experienced teacher has to say about resource corners and Differentiating Instruction

> *This differentiation is exhausting, frustrating, and time-consuming – but I would never go back to the old way.*
>
> From an experienced teacher
> (downloaded from the website)

4. Contextualising the Larger Societal Context with Reference to the Individual with SLD and the Educator

If we are to look at the child according to the Systemic Model or Bronfenbrenner's Ecological Model of Human Development – any individual or child is influenced and affected by a series of processes. Bronfenbrenner has conceived of these ecological environments as a set of four nested systems. In the case of a young child, one of the major *microsystem* may consist of the home environment with parents and siblings. Another important *microsystem* may be the school environment, with teachers and peers. The *microsystem* presents the links between the microsystems settings where the individual takes part directly i.e. the impact of home and school environment on each other. The next system is the *exosystem* in which the individual does not take part, directly but which affects the individual indirectly. For example, the parents' own background, ideology and aspirations or even the parents' work environment. Even the amount of technology in the parents' work environment will affect the child indirectly. The last setting is the, 'macro-system'. This relates to the general organisation and ideology of the society of which the individual is a part. Thus, each layer has three major dimensions, namely, physical space and materials, social roles and relationships and the individual's activities. Thus, the child's development depends upon a highly complex product of whatever qualities the child herself/himself brings to the system, as well as the interactive effects of all the layers in this system.

Bronfenbrenner argues that the best schemes for the overall development of a child are those that involve the families, since those that focus on the child alone tend to have only short-term effects. He argues that if parents are involved throughout they can sustain the effects after the programme is over. Bronfenbrenner's model demonstrates how changes in the macrosystem affects the exosystem and leads to changes in the child's mesosystem and microsystem. Hence, lies the importance of keeping in focus beyond the micro level while conceptualising and designing investigations. For example, as the larger macro-education thinking of our country moves towards accepting individuals who are differently abled,[4] acceptance of instructional differentiations within the classroom become possible and the individual's acceptance of self with variation and still an important contributing member of society becomes possible.

Contextualizing oneself in the larger societal context as a teacher and a teacher educator or a parent, one needs to introspect why I as a teacher is unable to provide the type of inputs to my class children who learn differently. Answers to this will also depend upon how strong is my understanding of myself as me the person and me the teacher as also my needs, aspirations, strengths and limitations.[5]

5. Being an *Effective Classroom Manager*

Facilitating support for children with specific learning difficulties also involves understanding and eliciting the best out of each and every child in the classroom. This requires the classroom facilitator (read as teacher) to be an effective classroom managers skilled in areas such as 'Encouraging Engagement' and continuously attempt to evolve his/her capacity of 'Withinness', ability of supervision and conduction of many simultaneous activities as also overlapping activities. They utilize instructional scaffolding and classroom movement management. Above all they preserve students' dignity to the maximum and avoid arguments. They follow through with brief interventions.

The child with SLD is at par with certain neuro-developmental constructs with relation to one's peergroup, in some the child may be way ahead while in still others the child's processing of those concepts and the output may be very different from the rest of the peer group. Thus, the teacher of the inclusive classroom needs to be effective in ones ability to provide "vertical enrichment" as well as "alternative enrichment" activities along with encouraging peer mentoring. While making the curriculum engaging for ones entire spectrum of students the teacher needs to be also sensitive towards how to negotiate specially amongst one's students with special needs their anger, projections, depressions, their conflicts and stresses.

For example, it is said that the most consistent thing about a child with SLD is the child's inconsistency, how will I manage this child who 'changes' almost everyday?

6. Development of Support Systems: Parent-Professional Collaborations

Education does not take place in a vacuum. The learner is not a machine wherein direct inputs and output systems work. The learner needs not only the support of the education system but of the family and the larger society. The teachers and the other education personels are the one's with expertise in the process of transaction of the knowledge bases. Hence initiation of the process of parent-professional collaborations lies on the shoulders of the education system. The stronger is the understanding of the basic issues between the family and the school, better will be the Human Support Systems of the learner. Such a system would facilitate the child to arrive at a realistic understanding of one's strengths and limitations as well as better transaction of effective strategies to learn and learning to learn.

It needs to be realized that the family system consists not only of parents but also siblings, grandparents, aunts and uncles neighbours and neighbourhood peers and friends while the education system consists of not only the class teacher but also the class friends and others teachers, non-teaching staff and the administrators.

Reassuring the parents and helping them evolve a support group will help them come to terms with the issue. With the support of parents, an individualized daily checklist and other instructional support systems are being developed for the child with parent-professional collaborations. The process of softly weaning the child towards independent living and decision-making if done with parental collaborations has longer lasting effects. Once the parents are able to understand and become partners in the process, it has been observed that they tend to gain so much of insight that they become the experts in the area.

7. Diagnostic Labelling: Of the Person or the Construct?

Children who learn together learn to live together.

Inclusion begins from the beginning of the education system. There are certain nursery schools where the children just know one has to help each other. They know that you do not have to go out of your way to help the child who comes to class with clutches with his arithmetic, but you may get a glass of water for him when you go to get one for yourself. But for another child you must be patient when he/she cannot put a easy zigzaw together but he/she can very well go and get his/her glass of water himself/herself.

Here are some narratives collected from children from different regular schools, who have friends in their schools who are children with SLD.

> *"He will continue to make mistakes with carry over sums for a very long time. If he had to do only and only that sum he does not make that many mistakes. I can manage many takes together. But he is so good with the casio."*

> *"It is not that she does not know the nitrogen cycle ma'am. It's just that it does not come out neat on her copy. Wish they could test her in some other way. She knows many things that other children do not know."*

I : Child you are missing your study time to be a scribe for this child.

Scribe from class VII: Ma'am this is also very important. We must learn to help each other.

Another Scribe: I want to become an IAS. I must understand the different type of problems and different type of people in this world.

Here are some comments as to how a larger labelling does not necessarily get to the root of the problem specially in the case of individuals with SLD. Every individual with SLD is different from other individuals with SLD and yet they have certain commonalities. Rather than a holistic labelling, it is better to understand the particular construct which needs to be addressed.

Child with Dyslexia: How do you want me to read? The way I understand or the way I am supposed to read in class?

Child with Dyscalculia: I really want to be an astronaut. (Brings down his voice to almost a whisper) Aunty!! You know I know much more than the topper of all the sections Who is to believe me?

Child with SLD: Oh!! Only if I could get through the competitive exam. I CAN DO IT.

8. Family Therapy Approaches Versus Individual Therapy Approaches

Family therapy evolves around the philosophy that any changes that one may attempt to bring about in an individual will depend upon the networking and requisite change in dynamics within the larger family. In family therapy, the entire family and extended members involved with the individual are a part of the therapy. Here are some examples of how the confidence and alternate learning processes of this child will be effected if the larger family is not sensitive to the issues of the child with SLD.

Parent : When all the relatives get together, and the children are together, it becomes so difficult to hide that she is not doing well in school.

Relative: There is this niece of mine, her parents are so worried. She just does not want to open her books. I have counseled her also. The school says do not force her to study too much. But if she does not study how will she get into any competitive examinations.

Parent: I wanted to go and thank the school. But its two years when he finished his class XII, I just have not been able to do it. There are so many bad memories. I do not blame him for not wanting to go back to meet his teachers. He says he might just land up slapping some of them – atleast especially one of them.

Relative: All children of our family are good in studies. 'Patha nahi yeh kaha se bade ho gaya?'. One does not know where is he born from?

9. Encouraging the Individual to be an Advocate of Ones Strengths

Children with multiple disabilities may also have specific learning issues, but generally the child in the regular classroom with learning difficulties is above average or average in intelligence and many of them with strong bend towards creativity. They tend to have more strengths from the right brain. Hence as the child grows and matures, it has been seen that the child needs to be made to understand where their strengths and limitations lie. Studies in the Indian context highlight that even peers of children in the pre-adolescent period when asked tend to highlight the strengths and limitations of child with disabilities. They generally do not label them. It is the adults in the children's life who find it easier to put information into categories and hence the process of labelling becomes more and more rigid. Here are examples from the narrations of some of the children who have been identified and certified as dyslexic, dysgraphic and dyscalculia and have been provided support by CBSE. Simultaneously their school and family had taught them to negotiate for themselves and focus towards enhancing their strengths.

> *I can spell really large words accurately; my problem is with understanding where to use the correct vowels.*

> *I know my multiplications and divisions well, but the problem comes when the numerical is given in the form of a paragraph. It's my reading which is bad and not my maths concepts.*

> *When people around me are talking or even whispering I find it difficult to concentrate and hence a seat near the window is just not a good idea for me. I also need breaks very often. I cannot be at a task for too long.*

> *I have a problem with directionality and hence I find it difficult to get my physics numerical from the chapter on speed correct or for that matter even some of the geometry theorems. Wish they would give choice between algebra and geometry in the examinations.*

> *I can think up a storyline well and narrate it to you but putting it on paper is not my strength. Although I plan to direct plays but getting into English (Hons) or journalism may be difficult for me. I have heard that there is a software that converts talk into the written word, I plan to learn how to use that.*

Although I have cleared the BBA entrance examination, but I went and saw the college, they have just one OHP for the entire college and so the teaching will be only chalk and talk. That is not good for me. I am looking for some place which will use more of audio-visuals.

Sir! Can I get an inside room in the hostel. Too much of movement of people coming and going is highly distracting for me than it is for most people.

10. Encouraging Team Building

Collateral and cooperative learning are important means of not only learning but also getting along with others and clubbing the strengths of different individuals together in order to reach similar desirable goals. Below is the example of a child with specific learning disability whose school and family environment provided opportunities for learning to work in a team and another was not given the requisite advantage of learning to work with teams. At the college level, their peer and the adults in their respective professional internships accept both these individuals with dyslexia so differently. Team work involves:

- Delegations of duties
- Taking up respònsibilities
- Highlighting strengths
- Using alternate resources
- Sharing the information
- Consolidating the information to complete the project.

Both the young adults have been working on their research projects in a team and are expected to complete and submit a report of the research as a group.

Amit is aware that he is not good at comprehension and at writing a summarization. He has negotiated with his team members that he will surf the internet and bring back as much information of relevance to the group. He will help in putting together the themes for the development of the questionnaire. He will go and administer the questionnaire to more than the number of people allotted to him if required. He can also do the tabulation of data effectively. What he informed his team is that he is not very good with analysis and drawing conclusions, sitting in the library and taking out requisite references and putting the questionnaire in the correct format. Hence the team saw this as extremely postive because Amit volunteered to do work instead of him as a liability to the team. Amit also keeps a little notepad where he jots down point for him to remember. (It is another matter, his handwriting being bad, he often is not able to read what he has written himself). Intuitively Amit at times realizes that the group is not happy with his efforts, he is learning how to tell them what all he did and that he is sorry he could not get the required outputs. Amit is accepted as an important member of the team.

On the other hand Geeta, does not really understand her strengths. Her teammates say that she has a lot of knowledge and it is a pleasure in one's free time to sit with her and listen to the insights she can give you on different topics. Her teammates' problem is that what ever task you give her she will not complete it. They think she is a 'shirker'. When Geeta is not able to complete a task she looks at it as a failure, finds it difficult to admit that she was not able to do it as it is not her strength. She makes excuses, which her teammates are able see as, 'half baked lies' and they get more and more upset with her and so does the faculty-in-charge. Geeta ultimately absent herself continuously on the most crucial days and leaves the group in even more difficult situation. She has started to lose friends and support in large leaps. You can observe that she is desperately waiting for the year to end so that she can move away.[6]

These examples were of advocacy or rather negotiation of one's strengths and delimit ones limitations. Advocacy also means being able to assertively and not aggressively insist that I have the provision of being provided a scribe and being able to request the invigilators not to speak loudly in the examination hall because it is even more distracting for me than for others.

11. Understanding the Learning Styles of Each and Every Child in the Classroom

Pedagogical issues do not emerge from the point the child enters the formal education system, rather they are present from the time the child commences his/her life. The teaching learning processes that the parents had been exposed to influence the way they interact with their child. The type of achievement orientations and aspirations that had governed their lives are translated to the child. Hence when the school system receives a child, the child is not a *tabula rosa*—as the hereditary and the environment already left its mark on the life pattern of the child. Hence when effective educational systems attempt to elicit the best out of the child with them, they work in partnership with the family of the child. In a country such as India where the influence of the extended and joint family systems still remain strong, the effective classroom teachers, counsellors administrators try and understand the family systems of the child when they are attempting to understand the child.

No educational systems can deny the construction of knowledge for the child or the individual. Individuals construct knowledge by their own ways. All that any educational system can do is to provide a facilitating environment at the appropriate maturational level of the individual. Different children learn by different means. One may be an auditory learner, visual learner, Kinesthetic learner, global learner or a combinations of any of the above. Hence in any classroom different children have different learning styles by which they learn best. Similarly in any classroom different teachers have different teaching styles and the different teachers teach best in their own particular way. Multimedia and other technological inputs not only support multi-sensory and multi-methodology teaching learning processes, they enable better conceptualization of concepts and ideas.

When a teacher is teaching she/he teaches with the assumption that the children are learning or rather constructing knowledge in a similar way as to what she/he had done when she/he had constructed that knowledge for themselves. But the way the individual with SLD's brain is wired is very different from the way that teacher's brain is wired or that of the larger population of individuals brain is wired. Or in other words the way the SLD child perceives the environment is very different from the way most teachers and the fellow students perceive the environment and hence the path that this child takes to arrive at the solution is very different. Now when the teacher attempts to use clues and supports and scaffolds in the classroom she does it in the way that she/he had learnt and had been taught and perceives that everyone learns that way. Hence the first step for the teacher is to be sensitive to the fact that each child learns differently and more so the child with SLD. The same sequences and steps to derive a concept may not necessary apply for this. As the child with SLD grows and matures she/he is often able to state how she/he learns best. Parents are often encouraged to follow the strategies for learning that the child wishes to use.

When one uses multi-sensory approach and multi-sensory instructional material the teacher automatically takes care of a variety of learning styles and it is but obvious if the same knowledge is received by the child in a variety of ways. The chances of the child's understanding and accommodating it into one's cognition is enhanced greatly.[7]

12. The Concept of Multiple Intelligence

Many of these children are gifted, talented and highly intuitive. Such individuals are faced by double problems in our highly categorized knowledge constructs. A 2e (twice exceptional) child is cognitively gifted but can't take in enough information due to auditory, visual, or sensory processing issues. It is like an adult in grade 7. i.e. curriculum too simple, but difficulty lies in taking in 'so' much of information non stop through the day, class after class. The contemporary theories of multiple intelligences such as Gardner's theory, point towards the need for vertical and alternate assignments and activities within the same classroom. This goes back to the need for resource kits and resource rooms within all educational system-school, colleges and universities.

One may conclude that a classroom may be made as, 'SLD friendly', as possible, but if there is no, 'SLD friendly teacher', and no, 'SLD friendly administrator' then nothing will happen.

REFERENCES

Ahluwalia, H.P.S., (2003). *Disability Status in India,* New Delhi, Rehabilitation Council of India.

Bos, C.S. & Vaughu, S. (1994). *Strategies for Teaching Students with Learning and Behaviour Problems.* Boston, Allyn and Bacon.

Brayan, T.H. & Broyan, James, H. (1986). *Understanding Learning Disabilities-3rd* ed. California, Mayfield Publishing House.

Cramer, S.C & Ellis,W. (ed) (1996). *Disabilities: Lifelong Issues,* London, Paul H. Books.

Edger, S. 1979, *The Psychology of Education – A Pedagogical Approach.* London: Methuen.

Farnham-Diggary, S (ed). (1978). *Learning Disabilities: Psychological Perspectives.* Cambridge, Harvard University Press.

Harding, L. (1986). *Learning Disabilities in the Primary Classroom.* London, Croom Halm.

Higgins, J. *et al.* (2003). *Practical Ideas that Really Work for Students with Dyslexia and Other Reading Disorders.*

Karanth, P. & Rozario, J. (ed) (2003). *Learning Disability in India: Willing the Mind to Learn*, New Delhi, Sage Publication.

Lamba, R. (2007). *Inclusion in Schools of Delhi: A Kaleidoscopic View*. New Delhi, Technical Series 3, Lady Irwin College.

Learner, J.W. (1988). *Learning Disabilities: Theories, Diagnosis and Teaching Strategies – 5ed.* Boston, Houghton Mifflin Company.

Malaviya, R. (2000). *Learning-Teaching Strategies for the Learning Disabled Child (Dyslexic) in the Regular Classroom.* In Sapra,R. Child Development. New Delhi.

Malaviya, R. (2006). *Creating a Learning Environment: Pedagogical Issues and Child Development.* New Delhi, Academic Excellence Malaviya, R. 2007. Disparate Learners: Common Goals, Personal Potentials, in Khanna, K. *et al., Vision for Teacher Education – Words in Gold,* New Delhi. Academic Excellence.

Overton, T. (1992). *Assessment in Special Education: An Applied Approach*, New York, Macmillan Publishing Company.

Rourke, B.P. & del Dotto, J.E. (1994). *Learning Disabilities: A Neuro-Psychological Perspective*, New Delhi, Sage Publication.

Rourke,B.P. & Doto, J.D. (ed) (1994). *Learning Disabilities: A Neuropsychological Perspective.* London, Sage Publication.

Smith, D.D. & Luckasson (1992). *Introduction to Special Education*, Boston: Allyn & Bacon.

Strichart, S.S. (1993). *Teaching Study Strategies to Students with Learning Disabilities.* Boston, Allyn & Bacon.

Susan, A. (ed) (1992). *Educational Alternatives for Students with Learning Disabilities.* New York, Spring-Verlog.

Thukral, E.G. (2002). *Children in Globalising India: Challenging our Conscience.* New Delhi, HAQ: Centre for Child Rights.

Williams, P. & Parker, J. (ed) (2006). *Social Work with People with Learning Difficulties*. Exeter, Learning Matters.

Kusuma, A. & Reddy, G.L. (2002). Management of Children with Learning Disabilities, *Disabilities and Impairment* Vol. 16(2), pp. 119-122.

NOTES

1. My own experience with attempting to teach spelling while try to put myself in the child's 'mental foot' has lead to my spellings getting effected and at times I land up spelling a word the way the child used

to. The child now spells the word the way society wants him to spell it. The child has been saved the agony of being called different and not intelligent by society. So much for societies and especially educators' mindset of insisting on watertight compartments of knowledge construction. Is it worth it?

2. Of course, there is this debate about mainstream from whose perspective!!, yet let us not go into that at this forum.
3. Such as child would be diagnosed and labled as dyslexic or dysgraphic or dyscalculia, depending upon other accompany constructs.
4. About two decades back the teacher educators at large, many school principals and the public definitely were not open to the idea that an individual could not read or write inspite of schooling and still become a novelist or a person who had problems with simple arithmetic could actually be able to run entrepreneurship with large-scale money transactions.
5. As a go along in my profession my mindset that all people in the caring professions such as teachers, doctors, nurses, counsellor, social workers and so on need to be put on the provial Freudian Couch in order to let go of some of their biases and to understand the biases that they are unable to let go off.
6. Geeta has information but does not know how to share it appropriately. She is highly disorganized but good at convincing people. She has good verbal skills.
7. Children with dyscalculia or acalculia are often able to arrive at the answer of a numerical but not in the process that is expected by the education system. One may find them with the answer scribbled at the back of the answer sheet and at times they get caught and are not able explain that they have not been cheating. Similarly children with SLD are supposed to be made to sit in a place with minimum of distractions. Hence, the school principal or counsellor may give direction to the examination in-charge to make all the children with SLD sit in a separate room. In may a school they land up being made to sit in the room, which acts as the examination centre. Now that room during the examination time has maximum movement and noise. Just because all the teachers are not sensitive to the needs to a SLD child instead of decreasing the extra stimuli, it gets increased manifold. On top of that the subject teacher may skip coming over and providing the requisite instructions, which she/he did to the other student of the class, who are sitting together let alone providing any permissible extra support to the child.

11

Employment of the People with Disabilities: Some Reflective Suggestions

Dr. Ashwani Aggarwal

Today, I would like to discuss, based on my experiences as a visually challenged person, about meeting the vocational aspiration of people with disabilities (PWD). I would share those experiences I faced myself with the text-based education. Next, I would share my experiences of National Association for the Blind as the joint secretary of this association. Further, I would like to present the do's and don'ts of and for the rehabilitation experts as trainer working with Punjab National Bank.

My experience tells me that there is a possibility of moving from philosophy of child deficit to a philosophy of environment deficit model while conceptualizing Inclusion. This would shift the focus from the child to enabling environment for inclusion. Next step would be to empower the child as well as the environment for a most cohesive setting. This is exactly what the National Association for the Blind (NAB) is attempting to do. NAB is working in those areas, which has not been explored earlier for people with challenges.

NAB has been able to successfully include people with visual challenges into a whole spectrum of professional areas. The following list is only indicative of various professional areas in which people with visual challenges have been successfully included:

Computer Programming

- Technical Education,
- Voice modulation and call centre,
- Office Administration,

- Master of Business Administration (MBA) from leading institutions.
- Cost Accountancy.

The most obvious question here would be what did we use do to achieve this. We believed in ourselves, break all the attitude barriers, thought differently (inclusively) and opened up the flood-gates of opportunities for all.

I have a questions for this group. At what age do you think a child with disability should begin to learn computers specifically if it's a blind child?
Audience : 3 years old.

Absolutely. Child starts using computer and key-board at a very early ages. But instead of providing the resources ourselves we wait for things to happen by someone else and then we blame that people are not competent.

How to make work place accessible and better job profiles feasible for people with disability is a major challenge for any rehabilitation programme. One after hears conversations in the field of work about the perceived need to have more PWD teachers and managers. But one can assess the numbers merely by looking around as whether it is this university of the other organizations to which we all belong to the number of people with disability is quiet less. For one reason or the other their competence has been questioned. The organization starts with the best of intention but often end up with few or no people with disability at managerial and supervisory position or as teachers. How is it that so many agencies recognize the need for competent people with disability role models as essential yet fall short of the marks?

The answer is not simple and the cure would not be easy.

As rehabilitation experts we are often told that treat them as equals, they are not different. But do we really believe in that? The attitude is a major guideline. Do we have to work for people with special need or work with people with special needs?

As with most pervasive problems, weeding out the underlying negative behaviour will take much through and time.

The unfortunate fact is that many professionals in the field of work with the PWD became interested because of their desire to help others i.e., the ablebodied wanting to the help the disabled. One side of the equation is able and the other side isn't. At an emotional level they remain the people to be helped and at a professional level as helpers. Society in general would not be able to accept people with disabilities as equals as long as such attitudes prevail.

With few exceptions, formal educational programmes at school as well as higher level make little or no effort to cull not out people with this attitude. Besides, they might respond, what's wrong with training people for the field who want to help those who are less able than themselves? Can't people be educated over time to understand that people with disabilities are their equals? Can't this underlying caring be converted into useful energy to help people with disabilities matriculate into all level of society? My answer is: usually not. It is very difficult to change what, for lack of a better phrase, I shall call primary motivations. If a person's initial attraction to the field of disability is to help the less fortunate, it is like to require passing through the dark night of the soul for that person to come to see people with disabilities as normal folks, as colleagues on the road to adult self-realization. Unless he or she come to a true recognition of these motives and develops the willingness to reshape them little progress will be possible, and the *status quo* will be perpetuated.

This problem is seldom expressed openly; in fact, most agencies cling to the assumption that we professionals have been trained and understand that people with disabilities are our equals. Agency personnel take years to believe that we are all singing form the same hymnal when in fact we are not. Attempts to hire competent people with disabilities always seem to run into road-blocks. Managers just can't find any people with disabilities who they believe are good enough. There always seems to be some reason why a particular person with disabilities just doesn't measure up. Somehow no people are ever available when the agency needs them. And there is never time to focus on the problem. There is no strategy to empower people with disabilities.

The group will agree with me that if they introspect in their organizations they will find that in their staff the selection bodies have not selected people with disability and if they have it is not more than one/two to whom we term as exceptions.

In most organizations the fact remains that people without disability or people with disabilities with poor skills are hired and promoted for what seem like perfectly rational and logical reasons, and the existing problems and behaviours are perpetuated and reinforced.

I will make one final observation before moving on. All this usually happens with the best of intentions and complete good will. Nobody sets out to harm people with disabilities, limits their involvement, or keep them underemployed—infact exactly the opposite is true. Though the results may not be positive, the intentions are truly laudable.

Rather than looking at the leaves on the tree, we needs to look at the roots to understand why things are the way they are. In discussions among agency managers one hears a sense of real frustration. "We hired this PWD guy to manage our programme, and, though he talked a good game, it turned out that he didn't have good skills of PWD and wasn't able to travel on his own or accomplish tasks in a timely manner. Now we have to keep him because he is our only PWD manager, and how would it look if we fired him? This kind of hiring is usually the result of a very narrow search. The agency looks through the list of the PWD people it knows best—its past clients. They hire somebody, hoping against hope that thing will work out, but they usually do not. Again the agency manager could say, "Something must be wrong with my methods," but unfortunately (and more likely) the manager will conclude, "There just aren't many competent folks outs there." So how is it that some programmes have high numbers of competent PWD staff at all levels? How do they manage to have a large cadre of PWD people waiting for the opportunity to work in their programmes? The simple truth is that successful leadership teams are doing many things wrong. Here are some do's and don'ts to help programmes build a competent PWD workforce. These have been gleaned from my twenty years of work in and observation of pubic and private agency rehabilitation programmes and industries for the PWD.

1. Successful recruitment is an ongoing process, which begins before the need for employees arises. The time to recruit is not when you need someone. The odds that a qualified PWD person will be available and will apply for your job are not good. Competent managers should be developing lists of prospective qualified employees far in advance of their need. Attendance at conventions and college training programmes and tours of other rehabilitation programmes should be used as opportunities to identify those who are competent and to establish ongoing communication with them.
2. Good managers steal employees. It is always best to get a known quality person. Look at people who are doing work at other programmes, and get to know them. Almost everyone is looking for a job if given the right incentives. Figure out what those incentives are and lure new employees to your organization.
3. Associate with PWD people. Hang around enough folks, and you will spot the ones who have the skills you need or who can be trained to meet those needs.
4. Avoid hiring past clients of your rehabilitation programme as management staff or instructors until they have gone out into the working world and proven to themselves that they can be successful. Sometime during training every PWD person considers becoming a teacher of the PWD. This is natural. But, until they have been out there and learned for themselves that they really can be successful in the rough and tumble of the workplace, you don't want them serving as PWD role models.
5. Get to know PWD people outside the field of PWD rehabilitation. Thousands of folks working life in every walk of life might be persuaded to move into the PWD field. The nice thing about hiring a PWD personnel manager away from the local bank is that he or she is unlikely to be accepting your job solely to help the PWD. And you probably won't have to begin by eradicating lots of past bad work habits or attitudes about PWD before you can develop a proper perspective in them.
6. Hire PWD people who seem a little cocky to you. I don't mean people who are downright difficult to get along with. People like Helen Keller and Edison were path breakers and

those who could think differently. Successful PWD people have usually learned that, if they had listened to what others thought they could or should do, they would never have done much. The result is that they are just little cocky, occasionally breaking rules, and they have an underlying independent streak that most organizations say they want in managers. If you find such people a bit abrasive and therefore you tend to shy away from them, ask yourself if perhaps you are actually looking for managers who are yes-people and your preference for the easygoing is merely a symptom. Also consider the possibility that you prefer passive PWD people because that's the way you are used to having them behave.

7. Your goal as a director should be to reach a critical mass of competent PWD people. One or two PWD people with good skills in an organization can be written off as amazing individuals. Eight or ten, on the other hand, become the norm, and their behaviour becomes the standard for future employees. Reaching a critical mass is essential if training programmes are to be successful. When most PWD people come to agencies for training, they have a very limited concept of what is possible for them. If they are shown enough competent PWD staff, they will come to believe that competence is the norm. For the PWD as well as the people without disability, seeing is believing. Your goal should be to have enough compentent PWD people on staff that students will say, "If that person can do it, so can I." This realization usually comes only through consistent exposure to competent PWD people over a long period of time.
8. Another value gained from hiring competent PWD staff is that they will spot others and help you lure them into the organization. Their testimony will be far better than yours because the truth is that they are PWD and you are not. As directors and managers you have a role in charting the course of work with the PWD for the next generation. As the baby-boomers retire and new employees come into the filed, they will represent our legacy. In the human services arena you can make no more valuable contribution than to hire the best. Agency policy can and does change; funding goes up and down. However, the people you are hiring now will in

all likelihood be around for the next twenty-five years. Basing our hiring decisions on sound principles and demanding excellence will help make major change in our field, and you will be proud to have truly helped change what it means to be people with disabilities.

12

A Profile of Saburi (nee Balloons): Including the Excluded

Ms. Rashmi Paliwal

Equipping people with disabilities with the necessary skill set. Saburi (nee Balloons) has for more than a decade now been providing equal employment opportunities to persons with disabilities in its office and factory. Till date it has trained about 300 people on different tasks in garment manufacture of which many have found employment in the company itself (on tasks as given in the below Table) as it had, at any given point of time 10-15 per cent of its workforce comprising of people with disabilities.

Tasks and Levels on which Persons with Disabilities were Employed

Reception
Accounts assistant
Tailoring
Quality checking
Measurement checking
Button marking
Buttoning
Numbering
Polybag packing
Packing
Running errands
Fieldwork
Supervising
Hand embroidery
Thread cutting
Trimming
Repair of beadwork on sequined garments
Assisting in the accessory store

Working on Machines

Overlock machine
Feed-of-the-arm pressing machine
Side seam pressing machine
Collar point machine
Cuff turning machines
Roller fusing machine

We have a training centre in South Delhi, which equips people with disabilities with skills required in the garment industry. Some of these are:

- Tailoring on juki machine,
- Measurement checking,
- Quality checking,
- Thread cutting,
- Folding,
- Tagging, and
- Packing.

Advocating for mainstream training opportunities. Having been trying to sensitize a mainstream institute, ATDC (Apparel Training and Design Centre) in the garment industry also start training people with disabilities for the last 3 years, it has now been successful in the same. This year the institute has opened up for training people with different disabilities and has already trained 3 batches in its Delhi and NOIDA branches. More recently another similar effort has been made with NITRA (Northern India Textile Research Association) and the latter is also open to provide training to people with disabilities.

Motivating other garment exporters. We have also been able to sensitize other garment exporters to absorb persons with disabilities. As a result 38 exporters in Delhi and NCR region have employed persons trained by us.

Sensitizing brands. Quite a few reputed brands/retailers such as GAP, H&M, Adidas, NEXT and IKEA have now joined in to help us in reaching out to their suppliers to employ people with disabilities in their work units.

Promoting research work. It also provides infrastructure and technical support to students from various institutions for research studies to identify new tasks for persons with disabilities in the garment industry. As a result of these studies, 4 persons with visual impairment were trained to work on specialized machines and new tasks were identified for persons with low intellectual functioning in the factory. *As a follow-through to the research work, more people with visual and intellectual impairments have been trained or helped to find placement in companies.*

Research Projects

1. Feasibility of employing the visually challenged in garment manufacturing, Garg. C. and Kumar. P., Diploma project, Garment Manufacturing Technology Department, NIFT, 1998-2000.
2. Development of Training Module in Garment Manufacturing Process for Mentally Challenged and Visually Impaired: an attempt towards Gainful Employment, M. Madhu, Dissertation, M.Sc. Home Science, Department of Textiles & Clothing, Lady Irwin College, 2000-01.
3. Adapting the button stitching and button hole making machines using the principle of universal design, S. Amitoj, Indian Institute of Technology, New Delhi, 2002.
4. Rehabilitation of Orthopaedically Impaired Individuals in Garment Manufacturing Unit, Jindal. S, Department of Textiles and Clothing, Lady Irwin College, 2002.
5. Bharti, D and Mahajan, N: Potential of employing physically challenged in the garment industry, Garment Manufacturing Technology Department, NIFT, New Delhi, 2001-03.
6. Training Modules for Gaining Employment of hearing Impaired individuals in Garment Manufacturing Unit, Bhasin. J., Department of Textiles and Clothing, Lady Irwin College, 2004.
7. Development of Training Modules for Mentally Challenged for Employment in Garment Manufacturing Units, Manaktala., N., Department of Textiles & Clothing, Lady Irwin College, 2005.
8. Development of Training Module for Gainful Employment of Mentally Challenged Individuals in Garment Manufact-uring Units, Aggarwal, D., Department of Textiles & Clothing, Lady Irwin College, 2006.

9. Work-aids development for physically challenged sewing operators, Jain, V. and K. Mohit Garment Manufacturing Technology Department, NIFT, 2005-06.

Participation in industry specific exhibitions to promote the issue. From time-to-time, Saburi tries to convey this message to more people in the industry by participating in exhibitions. In two of such fairs GARTEX-2002, 2003, 2005 a team of workers with visual, hearing and orthopedic impairment demonstrated their skills on specialized machines used in the garment industry.

Advocacy at a macro level. Saburi participates in different public forums to share its successful experience as an employer of persons with disabilities. Some of these have been organized by NGO's working in the disability sector, others have been at DU, Lady Irwin College, Partners in Change, JNU, CII, FICCI. We have also travelled to places such as Ropar and Gwalior to share our experiences with other NGO's, corporates, and parents of persons with disabilities.

In August 2002, the company organized an event entitled *Promoting Employment Opportunity for Persons with Disabilities in the Garment Industry* in collaboration with NIFT. The event was widely participated by important stakeholders like garment exporters, NGO's, industry associations, government agencies, academic institutions and persons with disabilities themselves and helped to start a thinking process among the participants including the corporates.

In November 2002, it presented a paper in a conference organized by the *National HRD Network.* It has also represented the corporate sector in the state seminars of a premier disability advocacy organization, NCPEDP.

During the Abilities Mela-2005, it brought all stakeholders, namely—NGO's, exporters, academicians and individuals with disabilities to a common platform to discuss the issues regarding employment for people with disabilities.

In the year 2000-01, Saburi conducted a disability awareness campaign, consisting of a play "Hum Honge Kaamyaab" enacted by persons with disabilities, covering 20 schools, 2 colleges and a few public places. Similarly get-togethers with NGOs and corporate friends were organized in the factory premises. The events marked distribution of sewing machines, tricycles and wheelchairs to a few NGO's and individuals with a disability.

Case Studies of Two of Our Trainees

Mansoor Khan is a 19-year old boy affected with polio in both his legs. His family is a large one comprising of his widowed mother, who was the only earning member of the family after his father's death and 6 younger siblings to take care of.

In order to add on to his family's income, Mansoor started to learn tailoring in a local shop, along with his studies. Following the stint, he also worked in a small factory for a while when given an opportunity. In a year of skill training, he heard of the center equipping people for jobs in the garment industry free of cost. Mansoor soon joined the center to train on the hi-speed 'juki' machine. Each day he would start from his place, walking 'on his hands 'and reaching the stand to catch the shared autos that plied in the area. Further he boarded a bus till near the center and covered the rest of the distance walking. In the next 10 days he had picked up the basic working of the machine and was then sent to the Gurgaon factory for an industry exposure on the same, where he stayed with his uncle for one and a half months till he was ready to join the industry.

He was sent for trial to an exporter in Faridabad, where after proving his skill, he was given a job. Mansoor now manages to earn Rs. 8000/- each month, including his overtime benefits. Meanwhile, he has also continued his studies and is now pursuing his IInd year in college!

Puja Mathur is a 20–year-old girl, who on being exposed to high fever when she was 16 years, lost her sight. Puja had to leave studies till she and her family came to terms with the reality of the situation. Puja joined the NAB center for women to learn to cope without vision and to have some skill, which would help her in the future. Here she was trained, besides other life skills on diya making, paper bag making and also stitching. After a while NAB referred her to a training center where she would be trained on acquiring skills to join the garment industry. Puja was trained on packing and folding related tasks. After three months, she was sent for an industry exposure to learn at work, in a company which had gradually but steadily opened up to employing people with different disabilities in the last few years.

Though, there was still hesitation to take in a person with Visual Impairment, persistent efforts resulted in the company finally relenting to providing the exposure. While the NAB Centre for Blind Women supported her in mobility training (to learn how to travel to the place of work using public transport and tackling the roads independently), the training center helped her in adjusting to the work environment and also sensitizing and preparing the company staff for the same.

The initiative was successful as the company also gave total support to it so that following the exposure Puja was taken in as a full time employee in the packing department.

Ironically, the owner of the company had at one point of time few years back when introduced to the concept of employing PWD's had categorically conveyed that it was not at all possible for person with VI to work in the garment industry! The myth, after so many years, has now changed.

13

Conclusions

Dr. Vandana Saxena

Both the seminar presented a unique opportunity to discuss various facets of Inclusion. The participation of personnel with diverse experiences enriched the whole proceedings. Many issues were raised during discussion hours. Although the best advocates of inclusion possibly are those people who have experienced exclusion by themselves, yet the role of society and community at large cannot be undermined. Building such social institutions, which empower each member to contribute according to her/his abilities, would only create a more cohesive society.

Inclusion still is an evolving concept and the contemporary society is better prepared to advocate for, as well as develop appropriate provisions for the same. There are three major areas to focus upon:

- The Policy Perspective
- Community Sensitization
- Educational Provisions
- Vocational Opportunities and Professional Possibilities.

The Policy Perspective

Many policies have been formulated clearly announcing the commitment of the State to support inclusion (refer appendix). However, the implementation programmes need to be worked upon. Some such systems need to be evolved, which would automatically reinforce the implementation of these policies. Also there is need for collecting feedback constantly from the field and suitably modifying the policies to maximize their benefit for the larger number of people.

Community Sensitization

It is very difficult to decide the order between policy implementation and community sensitization. Which would follow what? Is it the policy that would initiate the process of inclusion or is it a more sensitive society that would accept inclusion? The role of family, neighbourhood and community cannot be negated at any point. When in school, the voices of all children are important. The media needs to promote goodwill amongst people. The fear of encroachment has to move out of people's life. We all have to stand together and univocally welcome each one of us to live in complete harmony with each other. It's more in the mind than in the environment. With better-nourished minds the challenges would be met more effectively.

Educational Provisions

To successfully achieve inclusion the educational practices should be suitably modified. A timely intervention would require inputs at many levels.

- Curricular provisions
- Infrastructural provisions
- Teacher preparation programmes
  (*Both at pre- service as well as in- service levels*).

Inclusion means enabling pupils to participate in the life and work of all types of institutions to the best of their abilities.

For it to be effective, regular school have to adopt multi-dimmensional approach to:

- The Curriculum
- Funding Mechanisms
- Physical Infrastructure.

Inclusion is still an evolving concept, but its benefits are recognized and now there is a clearer focus on how to change system, methodologies, curricula and environment to suit the requirement. Inclusion need not be restricted by large class sizes or a lack of material resources. Attitudinal barriers to inclusion are greater than economic difficulties. It is necessary to provide a supportive infrastructure and management. There is a need of in-service training programmes for all people in the system to make inclusion happen.

Broadening of skill required by teachers like knowledge about disabling conditions, assessment for diagnosis and planning, innovative teaching strategies for working with individual student, modifying curriculum in the context of mainstreamed curricula, innovative teaching-learning material and appropriate methodologies and lastly time management is the need of the hour. The existing scheme of Sarva Shiksha Abhiyan has a provision to include all children with disabilities under the umbrella of 'Education for All'. Therefore, the NGOs and other agencies should consume this provision to effectively include children with disabilities in school and also ensure that they are given education opportunities at par with non-disabled in the most appropriate environment as mandated by the PWD Act, 1995. For attaining this goal teamwork and conscious efforts are needed.

There is an ongoing and increasing need for useful resource materials and training courses on inclusive education. Also there is an urgent need to publicize and disseminate already existing useful documentation such as RCI Act, Persons with Disabilities Act, 1995 and Enabling Education Network (EENET Asia Newsletter is an important source of information, which promotes inclusive education in Asian countries and support closer collaboration).

'Inclusion' should be included as one of the compulsory papers in the pre-service teacher education programme to develop an understanding of inclusion as a human rights issue. Pre-service and in-service programmes should include curricular components that sensitize and equip the teachers for understanding and managing the needs of all children and thus ensuring equal participation by all in their classrooms.

A practicum paper should also be included in the pre-service programme on 'Inclusion' that may include project work in collaboration with NGOs working in this field.

The NGOs working in this field may be invited to familiarize the students of teacher education institutions on a regular basis.

Vocational Opportunities and Professional Possibilities

When occupational roles are acted out, when families discuss 'what do you want to be when you grow up' we forget to ask this question to a child with special needs (Sanyal S. 2007). If children with special needs are in an inclusive environment their aspirations would be similar to their peer group. It is important that transition plans be based on individual's strength and interest, rather than adult's perception about what children can do.

Economic independence and a feel of worthiness constantly boost up one's self-esteem. NGOs and other organizations should intensify their efforts to generate employment opportunities for persons with disabilities and work for their rehabilitation in all sectors of the economy.

Concluding Remarks

People with Special needs, probably, are the most disadvantaged and marginalized in our society, possibly because of our own incompetence to provide them with equal opportunities and appropriate work environment. To effectively address the issues related with inclusion the social, cultural and physical structures need to be debated. It is more an issue of realizing human unity where human dignity is respected. Working against the unjust practices and planning for actualization of equal opportunities for all, alone can take us towards a bright, harmonious and peaceful tomorrow.

APPENDIX–I

About Rehabilitation Council of India (RCI)

The rehabilitation of persons with disabilities in India has been receiving attention during the last five decades since independence. Hardly any planned efforts were made in this field for developing trained manpower which could help in rehabilitation of the persons with disabilities in India.

The year 1981 was declared as the 'International Year of the Disabled Persons (IYDP)' by the United Nations. This was a good and welcome beginning as it concentrated as a means to arouse public understanding and awareness as a first step before embarking upon a whole programme of activities which need to be spread over a period of years.

Lack of appropriate trained manpower has been one of the major constraints in the expansion of rehabilitation services in the country. The training programmes in the field of rehabilitation/special education were isolated and ad-hoc in nature, with no standard syllabi.There was no uniformity in the teaching curriculum run by various institutions at the Under-Graduate, Graduate and Post-Graduate levels. It was, therefore, decided by the Government of India in 1986 to set-up a Rehabilitation Council to be responsible for:

- *(i)* training policies and programmes;
- *(ii)* to standardise the training courses for professionals dealing with persons with disabilities;
- *(iii)* to grant recognition to the institutions running these training courses;

(iv) to maintain a Central Rehabilitation Register of the rehabilitation professionals; and

(v) to promote research in Rehabilitation and Special Education.

In order to give statutory powers to the Council for carrying out its duties effectively the Rehabilitation Council of India Act, 1992, was passed by the Parliament which came into force with effect from 22nd June, 1993. The Amendment in the Act in 2000 gave the additional responsibility of promoting research to the Council.

The Persons with Disabilities (Equal Opportunities, Protection of Rights and Full Participation) Act, 1995 has changed the earlier concept of welfare of the disabled to the demand of equal opportunities and empowerment. The promise of access to education to every child with disability casts a special responsibility on the Council to provide trained manpower for their educational, vocational and social integration.

RCI has recognised several institutions throughout the country, which are conducting RCI approved courses for manpower development in the field of rehabilitation and special education. The Council regularly organizes seminars/conferences/workshops at national and international level for upgradation of knowledge and skills of professionals.

More About the Council

RCI is the only institution which takes care of manpower development of different categories of professionals for comprehensive rehabilitation of persons with disability to meet the needs of their entire life cycle, i.e., physical and medical rehabilitation; educational rehabilitation; vocational rehabilitation; and social rehabilitation.

Objectives of the Council

- To regulate the training policies and programmes in the field of rehabilitation of persons with disabilities.
- To bring about standardization of training courses for rehabilitation professionals/personnels dealing with persons with disabilities.
- To prescribe minimum standards of education and training in the field of rehabilitation uniformly throughout the country.

- To regulate these standards in all training institutions uniformly throughout the country.
- To recognize foreign degrees/diplomas/certificates in the field of rehabilitation awarded by Universities/Institutions on reciprocal basis.
- To maintain Central Rehabilitation Register of professionals/personnel possessing the recognised rehabilitation qualifications.
- To collect information on regular basis, on education and training in the field of rehabilitation of persons with disabilities from institutions in India and abroad.
- To encourage continuing rehabilitation education by way of collaboration with organizations working in the field of rehabilitation of persons with disabilities.
- To promote research in rehabilitation and special education.

How the Council Functions?

The Council Functions under the overall supervision of the General Council. The constitution of General Council as per the Act is as follows:

(a) a Chairperson, from amongst the persons having experience in administration with professional qualification in the field of rehabilitation, disabilities and special education, to be appointed by the Central Government;

(b) such number of members not exceeding seven, as may be nominated by the Central Government, to represent the Ministries of the Central Government dealing with matters relating to persons with disabilities;

(c) one member to be appointed by the Central Government to represent the University Grants Commission;

(d) one member to be appointed by the Central Government to represent the Directorate General of Indian Council of Medical Research;

(e) two members to be appointed by the Central Government to represent the Ministry or department of the States or the Union Territories dealing with Social Welfare by rotation in alphabetical order;

(f) such number of members not exceeding six as may be appointed by the Central Government from amongst the

rehabilitation professionals working in voluntary organisations;

(g) such number of members not exceeding six as may be appointed by the Central Government from amongst the medical practitioners enrolled under the Indian Medical Council Act, 1956 and engaged in rehabilitation of the handicapped;

(h) three Members of Parliament of whom two shall be elected by the House of the People and one by the Council of States;

(i) such number of members not exceeding three as may be nominated by the Central Government from amongst the social workers who are actively engaged in assisting the disabled; and

(j) the Member-Secretary, *ex-officio.*

The General Council is the supreme body and it functions with the help of an **Executive Committee** and various committees of experts drawn from different disciplines.

For professional and efficient functioning, the Council has set up a number of **Expert Committees** which meet regularly to consider all aspects of implementation of any programme, keeping in view the minimum level of standards to be maintained. These committees give guidelines for infrastructural facilities, faculty, their qualifications, equipments, etc., for various levels of programmes.

Various Expert Sub-Committees of RCI

1. Professionals in the field of Blindness and Low Vision.
2. Professionals in the field of Mental Illness and associated disabilities.
3. Professionals in the field of Leprosy Cured, Loco Motor and associated disabilities.
4. Professionals in the field of Hearing Impairment.
5. Professionals in the field of Multiple Handicapped.
6. Research and Fellowship.
7. Assessment and Accreditation Committee.
8. Advisory Committee.

ORGANISATIONAL CHART OF RCI

General Council

↓

Executive Committee

↓

Chairman

↓

Member-Secretary

↓

Sub-Committees/ Advisory Committees/ Zonal Advisory Committees

APPENDIX–II

The Persons with Disabilities (Equal Opportunities, Protection of Rights and Full Participation) Act, 1995

Introduction

"The Persons with Disabilities (Equal Opportunities, Protection of Rights and Full Participation) Act, 1995" has come into enforcement on February 7, 1996. This law is an important landmark and is a significant step in the direction to ensure equal opportunities for people with disabilities and their full participation in the nation building. The Act provides for both preventive and promotional aspects of rehabilitation like education, employment and vocational training, reservation, research and manpower development, creation of barrier-free environment, rehabilitation of persons with disability, unemployment and establishment of homes for persons with severe disability, etc.

This booklet aims at wider *dissemination* of the rights conferred *upon by* the Act.

Main Provisions of the Act

1. Prevention and Early Detection of Disabilities.
2. Education.
3. Employment.
4. Non-discrimination.
5. Research and Manpower Development.
6. Affirmative Action.
7. Social Security.
8. Grievance Redressal.

Prevention and Early Detection of Disabilities

- Surveys, investigations and research shall be conducted to ascertain the cause of occurrence of disabilities.
- Various measures shall be taken to prevent disabilities. Staff at the Primary Health Centre shall be trained to assist in this work.
- All the children shall be screened once in a year for identifying "at-risk" cases.
- Awareness campaigns shall be launched and sponsored to disseminate information.
- Measures shall be taken for pre-natal, perinatal and post-natal care of the mother and child.

Education

- Every child with disability shall have the right to free education till the age of 18 years in integrated schools or special schools.
- Appropriate transportation, removal of architectural barriers and restructuring of modifications in the examination system shall be ensured for the benefit of children with disabilities.
- Children with disabilities shall have the right to free books, scholarships, uniform and other learning material.
- Special schools for children with disabilities shall be equipped with vocational training facilities.
- Non-formal education shall be promoted for children with disabilities.
- Teachers Training Institutions shall be established to develop requisite manpower.
- Parents may move to appropriate fora for the redressal of grievances regarding the placement of their children with disabilities.

Employment

- Three per cent of vacancies in government employment shall be reserved for people with disabilities, one per cent each for persons suffering from:
    - Blindness or Low Vision.
    - Hearing Impairment.

- ❖ Locomotor Disabilities and Cerebral Plasy.

- Suitable scheme shall be formulated for:
  - ❖ The training and welfare of persons with disabilities.
  - ❖ The relaxation of upper age limit.
  - ❖ Regulating the employment.
  - ❖ Health and safety measures and creation of a non-handicapping environment in places where persons with disabilities are employed.

- Government Educational Institutes and other Educational Institutes receiving grant from Government shall reserve at least three per cent seats for people with disabilities.
- No employee can be sacked or demoted if they become disabled during service, although they can be moved to another post with the same pay and condition. No promotion can be denied because of impairment.

Affirmative Action

- Aids and appliances shall be made available to people with disabilities.
- Allotment of land shall be made at concessional rates to the people with disabilities for:
  - *(a)* House;
  - *(b)* Business;
  - *(c)* Special recreational centres;
  - *(d)* Special schools;
  - *(e)* Research schools; and
  - *(f)* Factories by enterpreneurs with disabilitity.

Non-Discrimination

- Public building, rail compartments, buses, ships and designed to give easy access to disabled people.
- In all public places and in waiting rooms, toilets shall be wheel chair accessible. Braille and sound symbols are also to be provided in lifts.
- All the places of public utility shall be made barrier-free by providing.

Research and Manpower Development

- Research in the following areas shall be sponsored and promoted:
  - Prevention of Disability.
  - Rehabilitation including CBR.
  - Development of Assistive Devices.
  - Job Identification.
  - On Site Modifications of Offices and Factories.
- Financial assistance shall be made available to the universities, other institutions of higher learning, professional bodies and non-government research units or institutions, for undertaking research for special education, rehabilitation and manpower development.

Social Security

- Financial assistance to non-government organisation for rehabilitation of persons with disabilities.
- Insurance coverage for the benefit of the government employees with disabilities.
- Unemployment allowance to people with disabilities registered with the special employment exchange for more than a year and who could not be placed in any gainful occupation.

Grievance Redressal

- In case of violation of rights as prescribed in the Act people with disabilities may move an application to:
  - Chief Commissioner for Persons with Disabilities in the Centre.
  - Commissioner for Persons with Disabilities in the States.

APPENDIX–III

Reservation of Jobs and Other Facilities for the Disabled Persons

(i) Three Percent Reservations in Grade 'C' and 'D' Posts

As per the order of Government of India reservation of 3 per cent in jobs have been made in Grade 'C' and Grade 'D' posts for the PH persons. The category of handicapped persons benefited are the blind, the deaf and the Orthopaedically Handicapped (O.H.) persons, as given below:

Category of handicapped	*Percent of reservation*
1. The Blind	1
2. The Deaf	1
3. The O.H.	1

For effective implementation of the reservation it has been advised to maintain a roaster of vacancies arising in Grade 'C' and Grade 'D' posts from year-to-year. The 34th vacancy may be earmarked for the blind. Similary the 67th vacancy and 100th vacancy would be reserved for the Deaf and the O.H. respectively in a cycle of 100 vacancies.

(ii) Definitions of Disabled for the Purpose of Reservation

1. ***The Blind*:** The blind are those who suffer from either of the following conditions:

   (a) Total absence of sight.

   (b) Visual acuity not exceeding 6/60 or 20/200 (Snellen) in the better eye with correcting lenses.

   (c) Limitation of the field of vision subtending an angle of 20 degree or worse.

2. *The Deaf:* The deaf are those in whom the sense of hearing is non-functional for ordinary purposes of life. They do not hear and understand sounds at all events with amplified speech. The cases included in this category will be those having hearing loss more than 90 decibles in the better ear (profound impairment) or total loss of hearing in both ears.

3. *The Orthopaedically Handicapped:* The orthopaedically handicapped are those who have a physical defect or deformity which causes an interference with the normal functioning of the bones, muscles and joints.

(iii) Identification of Jobs

In order to implement these reservations, without loss of productivity some posts are identified disability-wise.

To ensure sufficient recruitment of blind persons, separate list has been identified for the blind and partially blind persons.

(iv) Posting of Handicapped Candidates

As per the decision of Government of India Grade 'C' and Grade 'D' posts recruited on regional basis and who are physically handicapped may be given posting as far as possible near to their native place within the region subject to administrative constraints. PH employees may be given preference in transfer case near to their native place.

(v) Relaxation of Ban Order on Recruitment to Vacancies Earmarked far PH Persons

As per the Government order regarding ban on filling up of non-operational vacant posts will not be applicable in case of reserve vacancies to be filled up for PH person.

(vi) Carry Forward of Vacant Posts Under Reserve Category

As per the Government order if a reserve category of person is not available or the nature vacancy in an office is such that the given category of person cannot be employed then the post may be carried forward for a period of three subsequent years.

(vii) Appointment of VI Persons as Caner in Government Department]

As per the decision of Government of India it has been instructed that recaning of chairs in Government Offices should be done by blind persons as far as possible when the volume of work require a full time chair caner then a suitable post may be created in consultation with the Finance Department.

For the purpose of recaning the chairs in Government offices Vocational Rehabilitation Centres and Special Employment Exchange for the PH persons may be contacted.

(viii) Instruction to Appointing Authority for Intimating Vacancies Reserved for Handicap

As per the existing instruction of the Government all the vacancies in Grades 'C' and 'D' irrespective of their nature and duration are to be notified to the Employment Exchange and also to be filled through the agency unless filled through UPSC/SSC. It has also been decided that all the appointee should send their request to Employment Exchange/Special Employment Exchange/nearest Vocational Rehabilitation Centre for P.H. for nominating suitable handicapped persons.

(ix) Grant of Age Concession to PH Persons

As per the Government order it has been decided to extend the age concession of 10 years in favour of handicap persons to recruitment to posts filled through the SSC and through Employment Exchange in Grade 'C' & Grade 'D' posts.

(x) Relaxations in Typing Qualifications

As per the order PH persons who are otherwise eligible for appointment to posts of LDC but cannot be so appointed for being unable to satisfy the typing qualifications due to their disability may be exempted from the typing qualification for appointment.

(xi) Consideration for Confirmation in Job for Blind Persons

It has been instructed to all the Ministries/Departments of Government of India that there should not be any delay in confirmation of officers including blind persons on account of administrative delay. Ministry/Department should ensure, especially in which blind persons are employed that confirmation is made without delay and at appropriate time.

(xii) Reservation for PH Persons in Posts Filled by Promotion

As per the order handicapped persons may be promoted to Grades 'C' from 'D' and within Grade 'C' against the identified post if they are capable of being filled/held by the appropriate category of PH.

(xiii) Exemptions from Payment of Examinations Fee

As per the order PH persons recruited to Grade 'B' and Grade 'C' posts advertised by the UPSC and SSC will be exempted from the payment of applications and examination fee as prescribed by UPSC/SSC.

SPONSORSHIP POWER TO NATIONAL INSTITUTIONS

The Ministry of Labour in consultation with the Ministry of Social Justice and Empowerment and Department of Personnel and Training has decided to grant co-sponsoring power to the National Level rehabilitation institutes as given below:

1. National Institute for the Visually Handicapped, Dehradun.
2. National Institute for the Mentally Retarded, Secunderabad.
3. Ali Yavar Jung National Institute for the Hearing Handicapped, Mumbai.
4. National Institute for the Orthopaedically Handicapped, Kolkata.
5. National Institute for Rehabilitation Training and Research, Cuttack.
6. The Institute for the Physically Handicapped, Delhi.

APPENDIX–IV

The National Trust for Welfare of Persons with Autism, Cerebral Palsy, Mental Retardation and Multiple Disabilities Act, 1999

Objectives of the Act

This Act provides for the constitution of a national body for the Welfare of Persons with Autism, Cerebral Palsy, Mental Retardation and Multiple Disabilities. Such a national body will be a trust whose objects shall be as under:

(a) to enable and empower persons with disability to live as independently and as fully as possible within and as close to the community to which they belong;

(b) to strengthen facilities to provide support to persons with disability to live within their own families;

(c) to extend support to registered organisation to provide need based services during the period of crisis in the family of persons with disability;

(d) to deal with problems of persons with disability who do not have family support;

(e) to promote measures for the care and protection of persons with disability in the event of death of their parent or guardian;

(f) to evolve procedure for the appointment of guardians and trustees for persons with disability requiring such protection;

(g) to facilitate the realization of equal opportunities, protection of rights and full participation of persons with disability; and

(h) to do any other Act which is incidental to the aforesaid objects.

The Act received the assent of the President on 30th December, 1999 and extends to the whole of India.

Definitions

(a) "**autism** " means a condition of uneven skill development primarily affecting the communication and social abilities of a person, marked by repetitive and ritualistic behaviour;

(b) "**cerebral palsy**" means a group of non-progressive conditions of a person characterised by abnormal motor control posture resulting from brain insult or injuries occurring in the pre-natal, perinatal or infant period of development;

(c) "**mental retardation**" means a condition of arrested or incomplete development of mind of a person which is specially characterised by subnormality of intelligence;

(d) "**multiple disabilities**" means a combination of two or more disabilities as defined in clause (i) of Section 2 of the Persons with Disabilities (Equal Opportunities, Protection of Rights and Full Participation) Act, 1995. These are blindness, low vision, leprosy cured, hearing impairment, locomotor disability, mental retardation and mental illness;

(e) "**person with disability**" means a person suffering from any of the conditions relating to autism, cerebral palsy, mental retardation or a combination of any two or more of such conditions and includes a person suffering from severe multiple disability;

(f) "**professional**" means a person who is having special expertise in a field which would promote the welfare of persons with disability;

(g) "**registered organisation**" means an association of persons with disability or an association of parents of persons with disability or a voluntary organisation, as the case may be, registered under Section 12 of this Act;

(h) "**severe disability**" means disability with eighty per cent or more of one or more of multiple disabilities; and

(i) "**Trust**" means the National Trust for Welfare of Persons with Autism, Cerebral Palsy, Mental Retardation and Multiple Disability constituted under sub-section (1) of Section 3 of this Act.

Registration of Associations with the Board

Any Association of persons with disability or any association of parents of disabled persons or voluntary organizations can apply to the Board for registration. If application is genuine and is accompanied with necessary documents and fees, the association will be registered. Upon registration, the association can have access to or obtain copy of any book and documents maintained by the Board. The Board will determine the pre-funding status of registered organizations seeking financial assistance in accordance with regulations. The Board will also hold every year a meeting of registered organizations.

Local Level Committees

The Board will have to constitute Local Level Committees for different areas comprising of District Magistrate or the District Commissioner along with one representative from a registered organization and a person with disability for a period of three years to act as a Local Level Committee. These Local Level Committees have to meet at least once in three months.

Appointment of Guardians for Persons with Disability

A parent or relative of a person with disability may apply to the Local Level Committee for appointment of a guardian/or a person with disability. A registered organisation can also make such an application with consent of the natural guardian of the disabled person. The Local Level Committee will examine whether the person with disability needs a guardian and for what purpose and also lay down the duties of the guardian. The guardian will be responsible for the maintenance of the person with disability. The guardian will also submit to the Local Level Committee inventory and annual accounts of the property and assets, claims and liabilities in respect of such person with disability. A guardian so appointed can be removed for negligence or for misappropriating the property of the person with disability.

Source: Information and Guidance Booklet for Persons with Disabilities by RCI.
For further details visit www.rehabcouncil.org, www.socialjustice.nic.in, www.nationaltrust.org.in, www.ccdisabilities.nic.in

Index